Endorsements

What a pleasure it is for me to endorse my friend David Ravenhill's book, *Surviving the Anointing*. Reading through the pages of this book, I found myself at times deeply moved and challenged with a sense of soberness. *Surviving the Anointing* is probably one of the most timely and critically needed messages of our day....There is a battle raging for a generation and for the very soul of our nation, but we cannot win that battle without godly leaders of character who are equipped for longevity.

May you be provoked to a deeper level of consecrated commitment and to a higher level of expectation in Christ as you take to heart the message that David has clearly communicated in *Surviving the Anointing*.

Doug Stringer
Founder, Somebody Cares America/International
Turning Point Ministries International

The great missionary, Amy Carmichael, once said, "Can we follow the Savior far who have no wound or scar?" In the Church of the West, the anointing of God has become the needed badge for success and not much more. Little wonder then that thousands are falling by the wayside. Broken-hearted prostrations are reserved for the "spiritual nutcase," according to the Church of the 21st century.

Knowing David Ravenhill personally, I have seen him willing to sit in obscurity, filling his cup as the broken beggar. What more can be said of a follower of the Lamb than that he "followed the Lamb whithersoever He goest"! Seeing David's life I can truly see that God is once again raising up a voice in the wilderness.

—Kevin J. Turner
President, Strategic World Impact

Do you want to avoid shipwreck in your personal life and ministry? Do you want to avoid being yet another leadership casualty? Then this book is for you! Written by a senior statesman in the Body, *Surviving the Anointing* is as practical as it is convicting. It should be mandatory reading for everyone engaged in the work of the ministry.

—Dr. Michael L. Brown
President, FIRE School of Ministry
Concord, North Carolina

In a day when weaker men are preaching a watered-down gospel with little fire in it, David Ravenhill boldly steps forward with a compelling word for ministers. *Surviving the Anointing* is not for the timid; it is for those willing to pay the price to have an enduring ministry, filled with the power of God.

—Steve Gallagher
President, Pure Life Ministries
Dry Ridge, Kentucky

Surviving the Anointing

Learning to Effectively
Experience and Walk
in God's Power

David Ravenhill

Destiny Image® **Publishers, Inc.**
P.O. Box 310
Shippensburg, PA 17257-0310

*"Speaking to the Purposes of God for this Generation
and for the Generations to Come."*

For Worldwide Distribution, Printed in the U.S.A.

ISBN 10: 0-7684-2443-7

ISBN 13: 978-0-7684-2443-0

This book and all other Destiny Image, Revival Press, MercyPlace, Fresh Bread, Destiny Image Fiction, and Treasure House books are available at Christian bookstores and distributors worldwide.

For a U.S. bookstore nearest you, call
1-800-722-6774.

For more information on foreign distributors, call
717-532-3040.

Or reach us on the Internet:
www.destinyimage.com

1 2 3 4 5 6 7 8 9 10 11 / 09 08 07

Dedication

THIS book is dedicated to the numerous unsung men and women of God who have worked long and tirelessly in the work of the ministry—specifically to the many who have suffered years of imprisonment, separated from their families and flock, and yet have maintained a passionate devotion to their great God and Savior, Jesus Christ. Although their "labor of love" may never fully be known this side of eternity, they will, without a doubt, receive the ultimate reward when they stand before the Great Shepherd of the sheep and hear Him say, "Well done, thou good and faithful servant."

These spiritual giants are made up of tens of thousands of house church leaders in places like China, Sudan, Palestine, Iran, Iraq, and Cuba, as well as many other forgotten or little-known cities and locations. Joining their ranks are an innumerable host of national pastors and workers laboring in places like India, Africa, Burma, and Indonesia. Last, but by no means least, are those who have responded to the call of God and have left friends and family to travel to some foreign field. There they have learned a new language, adapted to a different culture, and have done it all for Christ and His cause.

These are the real heroes—men and women who will never grace the cover of some Christian magazine. No books or movies will ever be written or produced about their lives. They may never hear the praises of men or gain any earthly reward, yet they toil unselfishly, faithfully proclaiming the uncompromised Word of God while living a life of integrity before God and men. It has been my privilege to have known some of you. Others I look forward to meeting on that great and final day. Thank you for your godly example of servanthood and for your faithfulness. I salute you and honor you.

So Send I You[1]

> So send I you to labor unrewarded,
> To serve unpaid, unloved, unsought, unknown,
> To bear rebuke, to suffer scorn and scoffing;
> So send I you to toil for Me alone.
>
> So send I you to bind the bruised and broken,
> O'er wand'ring souls, to work, to weep, to wake,
> To bear the burden of a world aweary;
> So send I you to suffer, for My sake.
>
> So send I you to loneliness and longing,
> With heart a hung'ring for the loved and known,
> Forsaking home and kindred friend and dear one;
> So send I you to know My love alone.
>
> So send I you to hearts made hard by hatred,
> To eyes made blind because they will not see,
> To spend, tho' it be blood, to spend and spare not;
> So send I you to taste of Calvary.

Endnote

1. Song by Margaret Clarkson, published by Singspiration, Inc., 1954.

Contents

Preface

IN ancient Greek mythology there is a legend of two brothers, both of whom were well-known and respected architects. The king commissioned them to design and build a royal treasure house in which he could store his wealth. During the construction process they became increasingly possessed with a desire for King Hyrieus's treasure. Ingeniously they devised a plan to place one of the stones in a manner that it could be removed without the king's knowledge. So skillfully and meticulously was the work done that nobody except the two brothers had the slightest idea that the secret entrance existed.

After the completion of their work, they would from time to time remove the stone and enter the treasury to steal from the king's treasure. The king was amazed to discover that although his locks and seals remained unbroken, his treasure was slowly but steadily being depleted.

Many a man of God has experienced the same tragedy. While they have sought diligently to guard their lives in most areas, they have allowed one secret *opening* that has slowly but surely permitted the enemy to rob them of their spiritual wealth—their anointing.

Although King Hyrieus was unaware of the "secret stone," the same cannot be said for those in leadership. These secret sins are known both to God and the man or woman of God. Unless dealt with honestly and thoroughly, they will destroy both the person and his ministry.

How can these things be prevented? Please read on....

Introduction

I MAGINE that you have one of the most prominent titles and positions of authority in the largest and greatest kingdom in the universe. There are few, if any, apart from the Godhead who can even begin to compare themselves with you. You were created and prepared by God Himself for your position. From the beginning you knew that you had not achieved this by your own doing or willpower. Everything about you had been meticulously thought out in advance. You had been given wisdom and beauty of a kind that others can only begin to imagine. Finally you were assigned to "cover" God's greatest creation: man. For this task you were anointed, then placed in Paradise, the garden of God. Your name is lucifer the archangel.

Daily in the garden you witnessed God Himself coming in the cool of the day to talk and fellowship with His son, Adam and His daughter, Eve. You became jealous and coveted the honor, respect, and communion that man showed towards his Creator and Father. Desiring to be like God yourself, you appeared as an angel of light to Adam and Eve, subtly suggesting to them that they could also be like God...

But alas, your diabolical plan failed and you were *"cast...from the mountain of God"* (Ezek. 28:16). God cursed you above all the cattle of the earth...

You were *"the **anointed** cherub who covers"* (Ezek. 28:14). Let those words sink deeply into your spirit as you are reading this. You were, you *were*, you **were**, but you are no longer. The anointing has gone, along with everything you once possessed and were given.

Unfortunately, lucifer was just the beginning. Since then, tens of thousands have followed. Lucifer went from being the *"star of the morning"* (Isa. 14:12) to the "prince of darkness," from "favored" to "fallen." Since that time the devil has plotted, schemed, and deceived, seeking to settle the score. He is forever determined to take down any and all that he can.

The devil's trophy case is crammed full of "trophies" from every generation. His craftiness lured Eve from Paradise to prison. Solomon was seduced from his devotion to God to the worship of idols, despite his God-given wisdom and anointing. Saul began as God's first anointed king of Israel—he prophesied along with the other prophets—and yet he ended his life with these sad but poignant words: *"I have played the fool...I have erred exceedingly"* (see 1 Sam. 26:21). Saul sought counsel from a medium, then tried to take his own life. What a tragic ending to such a promising beginning. Samson began by terrorizing the Philistines, but in the end they tortured and taunted him. Esau sold his birthright for a bowl of "chili." Demas flirted with the world and left the ministry. Judas traded everything for some petty cash. The list is endless. I have personally worked with men whom I considered anointed servants of God, and yet I have watched as they have lost everything, shipwrecked their lives, never to sail again.

Just today I received an e-mail from a pastor and friend in Malaysia saying that he had resigned from his role of senior pastor due to moral failure. In his confession he says: "I know that many things we have dreamed about are now shattered."

Job expressed it this way: *"If my heart has been enticed by a woman...it would uproot all my increase"* (Job 31:9,12). As a wise man of God said years ago, *"When the house falls...great is the fall thereof"* (see Matt. 7:27); in other words, its effect has numerous ramifications that ripple across not only the local Church but also the Church at large.

It is imperative that we stop this needless "loss" of anointed men and women of God. Any military operation is bound to suffer some casualties—that's the very nature of war. America has been bringing home her wounded, not to mention the tens of thousands of "body bags," ever since engaging in her first war. Fortunately, something has changed in our two most recent wars: There's been a drastic reduction in the number of dead and wounded. This begs the simple question: Why?

Part of the answer lies in the fact that we are now better prepared. Not only do we have more sophisticated weapons, but also we have better intelligence concerning the "enemies devices."

Although this may be true in the natural realm, it certainly is not the case when it comes to spiritual warfare. God's army of soldiers are "dying" at a faster rate than ever before. According to John Maxwell, only one out of every ten people entering the ministry today will still be in it at the age of 65. That's a 90 percent dropout rate. Dr. James Dobson estimates that there are some 1,500 ministers a month leaving the ministry. If the Body of Christ continues to hemorrhage at this rate, we'll soon be the laughingstock of the world, not to mention the evil hordes of darkness.

As it appears now, the devil certainly seems to have gained the upper hand. Daily, it seems, we hear of another "fallen soldier."

The devil's strategy is both old and reliable: "Strike the shepherd and scatter the flock."

I have experienced firsthand the devastation caused by a man of God "falling." My wife and I assumed the responsibility of pastoring a congregation where the senior pastor had been involved in moral failure. The impact this had on the "flock" was horrific. Emotions ranged from anger to despair and everything in between. Another pastor told us it would take between five and eight years to restore trust and stability in the church—thankfully this was not to be the case.

In the early 1990s I sat listening to one of God's senior saints—a man who had and has experienced firsthand the mighty miraculous power of God in his life and ministry. (I've determined to learn all that I can from tried and true servants of God, people who have weathered life's storms, and stood the tests of time.) This man made a statement that will forever reverberate through my mind and spirit: "VERY FEW PEOPLE SURVIVE THE ANOINTING." Those words were spoken over a decade ago, yet they still carry the same impact now as they did then. I have determined by the grace of God to "finish the course" (see Acts 20:24; 2 Tim. 4:7).

The anointing can be compared in a crude way to winning the lottery. One moment you are poor, barely making it from day to day. You live in a very simple home with few luxuries; your car is in desperate need of repair; your clothes are few and well worn; and along with all of that, you have a mountain of debt. Suddenly all of that changes when you are informed that you have become the grand prize winner of some contest you entered—you are now worth millions! Within days of receiving your first check, you rush out and buy yourself a new home, fancy car, nice clothes, and so on. This new source of wealth gives you the ability to live the life you have always dreamed of.

The anointing has many similarities to that. God's grace or anointing transforms you from what you once were, into a person with the "ability" to do things you had previously only dreamed of. You now possess the ability to preach, teach, sing, and function in the realm of the Spirit through prophecy, healings, words of knowledge or wisdom, etc. But can you maintain this newfound "wealth"? Do you know how to steward this precious gifting and privilege?

An article in *USA Today* titled "Lottery Winners' Good Luck Can Go Bad Fast" tells the sad but true facts regarding individuals who have won and lost vast fortunes. Take for example "William 'Bud' Post who won $16.2 million in the Pennsylvania Lottery in 1988...Post lost and spent all his winnings. He was living off Social Security when he died in January." The article gives another example: "Two years after winning a $31 million Texas lottery in 1997, Billie Bob Harrell Jr. committed suicide. He had bought cars, real estate, gave money to his family, church, and friends. After his death it was not clear whether there was money left for estate taxes."[1] The article goes on to tell of others who have won and lost vast amounts of money.

Over the years, certain statements have left a powerful impression on my mind. I have mentioned this in one of my previous books, but nevertheless it bears repeating. I'm referring to a quote from a great teacher in the Body of Christ who said: "I do not want to be a shooting star." Let me explain that a little. Suppose you and some friends are outside on a clear night, maybe away from the city lights, and you look up to the heavens. You stand there and gaze on the multiplied millions of stars, each one different from the next. (I'm sure most of you have done this at one time or another.) Suddenly, as you're looking and admiring the stars, a meteorite streaks across the heavens, and somebody says, "Did you see that?" Momentarily everybody is enamored, captured by the spectacular burst of light as it streaks across the heaven. But within a matter of seconds it's gone, disappearing forever into the blackness from which it came.

There are men like that, women like that, who come on the scene for a brief period of time, great men of God, maybe everybody is reading their book, or everybody is listening to their tapes, or everybody is going to their conferences, and they seem to have the full attention of the Christian world—but tragically it is only for a moment and then they're gone and you say, "Whatever happened to that great healing evangelist," or "Whatever happened to that great teacher," or "Whatever happened to that great singer or songwriter?" Someone answers and says, "Oh him, he's turned his back on God," or "He divorced his wife, drifted off into some false teaching, or became involved in some type of sexual addiction." So very few people survive the anointing.

What you are about to read are some of the essential principles that I've gleaned over some 42 years of ministry. I have shared these principles with various leadership groups throughout the nation as well as around the world. It is my prayer that God will use this book to convict, challenge, change, and charge you as you seek to follow His will and purpose for your life and ministry.

I believe the principles that I will share in this book are essential to spiritual survival. As I mentioned earlier, over the years I have tried to look at and learn from great men and women of God—some of whom I've known or worked with personally—and I've had to take a good look at my own life, and have determined by the grace of God to finish the course. It's one thing to start; it's another thing to finish. Paul says, "*I finished the course, I've run the race, henceforth there is laid up for me a crown of righteousness*" (see 2 Tim. 4:7-8).

In my book, *They Drank From the River and Died in the Wilderness*, I tell of how one million people came out of Egypt.

They started the race, yet only two people out of that one million made it into the promised land. That's not a very large percentage—talk about not surviving the anointing! The Israelites were surrounded by the supernatural; they saw signs and wonders on a daily basis as God provided the manna for them to eat. They saw water flow out of a rock, and yet only two made it into God's purpose. And so we need to take heed.

Paul says, *"Lest when I preach to others, I myself should be disqualified to become a castaway"* (see 1 Cor. 9:27). This is not just for leaders, but it is for each and every one of us. And so I want us to look at some principles that I believe will help us to survive God's anointing.

As we begin this study, the very first thing I want to draw your attention to is First Peter 2:21. There it says, concerning the Lord Jesus Christ, that He left us *"an example...to follow in His steps."* So let's look at Jesus as *"the pattern son"* or, if you like, our role model. Throughout this book we will discuss some of the keys in the life of Jesus, and we'll start with: dependency. So let us begin.

Endnote

1. Oren Dorell, "Lottery Winners' Good Luck Can Go Bad Fast," *USA Today* (Feb. 26, 2006), accessed on the Internet at: http://www.usatoday.com/news/nation/2006-02-26-lotteryluck.x.htm.

Chapter 1

Dependency

> *O God, we have heard with our ears, our fathers have told us, the work that **You** did in their days, in the days of old. ... For by their own sword they did not possess the land, and their own arm did not save them, but **Your** right hand and **Your** arm and the light of **Your** presence, for **You** favored them* (Psalm 44:1,3 emphasis added).

God Wants Us to Depend on Him

THERE is no greater role model in the Christian life than the Lord Jesus Christ. Peter, in his Epistle, tells us that Jesus left "an example" for us and that we should *"follow in His steps"* (1 Pet. 2:21). Although the context for that verse specifically relates to suffering, nevertheless Jesus is our supreme example in all things. He is, in fact, the *pattern Son*. With that in mind, Jesus said in John 5:19, *"The Son can do nothing of Himself."* What an amazing statement! Jesus Christ, the Son of God, the Word that became flesh, in His earthly life says, "I can do absolutely nothing of Myself." The Son can do nothing apart from the Father.

In John 5:30, a few verses later, Jesus says, "*I can do nothing on My own initiative.*" In other words, "I don't initiate a single thing." Jesus did not practice "visualization"—the idea that if you can visualize something, it can become a reality. Many teachers today will tell you that if you can visualize a congregation of 1,000 people, then you can have it. (Poor Jesus apparently could only believe for 12.) No, He was totally dependent upon His Father. He said, "Whatever I hear the Father say, that's what I say. Whatever I see the Father doing, that's what I do. I don't do anything of My own free will" (see John 5). Basically He was saying, "I don't create anything. I listen. I'm totally dependent upon the Father."

In a later passage, as Jesus turned to His disciples, He said, "*Apart from Me you can do nothing*" (John 15:5). I believe that one of the major keys to longevity and continued blessing in the Christian life is to remain in the place of absolute and total dependency upon God. We must be absolutely convinced that:

1. "*In me* (that is, in my flesh) *nothing good dwells*" (Rom. 7:18 NKJV).

2. I do not have the ability, apart from the grace of God, to accomplish anything for the Kingdom of God.

3. I am totally and completely dependent upon Him for everything.

In Matthew chapter 5, Jesus went up a mountain and gathered together His disciples and began to teach them. His goal was to impart to His 12 future apostles an understanding of the Kingdom. He commences with the key to all other Kingdom principles by stating, "*Blessed are the poor in spirit, for theirs is the kingdom of Heaven*" (Matt. 5:3). That word "poor" is an interesting word in the Greek; it literally means "blessed are the *beggars*, for theirs is the kingdom of heaven."

Blessed Are the Beggars

In 1987 I went to India for the first time to teach for a week in a Bible school just outside the city of Hyderabad. One afternoon someone offered to take me on a tour of the city. This was my first real visit to India—apart from a brief touchdown once at the Bombay airport—and I was eager to experience its fascinating culture.

If you've ever been to India, you know that they use every available means of transport. There were horse-drawn carts, carts that were being pushed or pulled by people, bicycles, scooters, trucks, buses...just about every form of transport you could imagine. All these vehicles seemed to be piled up to Heaven, and the traffic appeared to have a mind of its own as it weaved among all the lanes. I was completely overwhelmed and absorbed with everything that was going on around me.

While waiting at a traffic signal, I heard a voice. I turned, assuming it was the driver, but it wasn't. The second time I heard it, I looked around again, and right beside me, sitting on a little median strip dividing the lanes of traffic, was a little boy, around 8-12 years of age. (It was hard to estimate his age due to his physical condition.) His body was all twisted, his arms were deformed, his legs were all knotted up beneath him, and he was begging.

I remember looking at that little boy and realizing: That's exactly what Jesus meant when He said, "*Blessed are the* [beggars], *for theirs is the kingdom of Heaven*" (Matt. 5:3). You see, that little boy had come to the realization that he didn't have the strength, he didn't have the dexterity or the mobility, to operate a machine or to do anything other than beg. Consequently, he was reduced to "surviving," if you like, on somebody else's generosity and goodness. In other words, his life was derived from somebody else's means, somebody else's wealth and graciousness. He was a beggar. He knew that he was not capable of managing by his own strength, and therefore he was reduced to a place of total dependency. If nobody helped him, he could not make it or exist on his own.

And that is the very first principle that Jesus gave concerning the Kingdom of God. If we are to be a part of God's Kingdom, principle number one is: "Blessed are the beggars." We have to be totally convinced that we have absolutely no ability in and of ourselves, and therefore see ourselves as beggars. I have told people around the world, and I am not ashamed to tell you, that I am a spiritual beggar. Hardly a day goes by that I don't get down on my face before God and lift up my tin cup, so to speak, and say, "God, give me of Your wealth. Give me of Your sustenance."

Notice the continuation of Matthew 5:3, which states, "*Blessed are the* [beggars], *for theirs is the kingdom of Heaven.*" It does not say, "for theirs *will* be the kingdom of Heaven." In other words, available to the beggar are all of Heaven's resources. What a beautiful statement. The Bible says, "*If any of you lacks wisdom, let him ask of God*" (James 1:5). God is a God who wants to provide in every area that you lack.

Even the apostle Paul asked: "*Who is adequate for these things?*" (2 Cor. 2:16). Can you imagine Paul saying that? Paul, one of the most brilliant theological minds, who had received his training under one of the greatest teachers of his day: Gamaliel. Paul referred to himself as a Pharisee of the Pharisees, his spiritual "pedigree" so to speak was a mile long, and yet Paul said, "I am not capable. I am not sufficient to effectively minister the gospel of Jesus Christ, but my sufficiency is in God Himself." Now if that's true of Paul, how much more is it true for you and I? And so God seeks to bring us to this place of dependency on Himself.

Prayer—Our Access to God

In Luke chapter 11 we have the disciples asking Jesus to teach them how to pray. My father used to say, "This is the only time anywhere in the New Testament where the disciples ever asked to be taught anything." There is no record of them saying, "Teach us how to preach." There's no record of them saying, "Teach us how to teach," or "Teach us how to walk on water," or even, "Teach us how to cast out devils."

One day the disciples did have a little bit of a problem, so they came to Jesus and said, "You know, yesterday we had no problem, Lord. The demons were just sort of popping out left, right, and center. But today, well, they seem to be pretty stubborn." And Jesus said, "Well, skip lunch and try again." That's my translation. The exact reply He gave was, "This kind does not go out except by prayer and fasting."

Nonetheless, when the disciples asked Jesus to teach them how to pray, it was the only time they actually said, "Teach us how to...."

You'll notice the passage says, *"While Jesus was praying...after He had finished..."* (Luke 11:1). And my father's observance, and I think he was right, was that they took notice that the key to the life and ministry of the Lord Jesus Christ lay in His relationship with the Father, and they saw that everything Jesus did was tied directly to the throne of God. They saw Jesus tapping in, so to speak, to the resources of Heaven, in prayer, making contact with God. And they said, "If You can teach us how to touch the throne of God, we can do what You do," in essence, "so teach us how to pray."

And of course Jesus gave them what we call the Lord's Prayer. In Luke 11:2-4 we have a shortened version of the Lord's Prayer that is found in Matthew 6:9-13. But in Luke's account we have something that we don't have in Matthew's account. After giving them the prayer, Jesus went right on to tell them a story. In Luke 11:5-6, Jesus said, *"Suppose one of you has a friend, and goes to him at midnight and says to him, 'Friend, lend me three loaves; for a friend of mine has come to me from a journey, and I have nothing to set before him.'"*

Now obviously the journey-weary friend arrived late at night, because the unprepared host goes to his other friend at midnight. So perhaps the visitor arrived around 11:30 p.m. This is a friend; the man has been expecting him; but he's failed to make preparation. Maybe he didn't expect his friend to get there until the morning. Maybe he knew the friend was coming from a great distance away and he thought, *Well, I'll have time to get up and go down to the local bakery and get some bread, and have it all ready.* Instead the guest arrives early and the man is embarrassed, because in this culture, as you probably know, providing hospitality was very important. You can imagine his embarrassment in not being able to meet his friend's need. He has absolutely nothing to give them.

But then he remembers that he has another friend, and the thing he remembers about this friend is that he always has an ample supply; he always has an abundance. So even though it's midnight, he goes to his friend's house and begins pounding on the door. And I can see his friend opening the windows saying, "Shhh, you're going to wake the baby. Don't you realize what time it is? The family is in bed; just leave me alone. What's going on? I'm not going to get up, so just leave me alone."

The man keeps on pounding, and eventually his friend knows he's not going to get any rest until he opens the door. Jesus says that his friend will "give him as much as he needs" (Luke 11:8).

Keep in mind that Jesus is speaking about prayer. You see, you and I will always be surrounded by friends, friends who have needs. They will come to us at some "midnight" hour or crisis in their lives with every type of need: emotional needs, spiritual needs, physical needs, marital needs, and more. Now the sooner we recognize that we have nothing to set before them, the better. This is the principle Jesus is teaching, "Of Myself, or by Myself, I can do absolutely nothing. I cannot solve your problem. But I have a friend who has the answer," and prayer is going to your greater Friend on behalf of your lesser friend, in order to get the answer. Our "friend" who art in Heaven....

Here's a situation: Maybe a couple's marriage is on the verge of breaking up, and they come to you two or three times, for counsel. You are at your wit's end; you don't know what to do next. You've tried. You've exhausted all your own abilities and wisdom, and so you get on your face before God and say, "God, I need an answer. This couple is coming again tonight. I do not have the 'bread.' I do not have the means to satisfy them, but You do, Lord. You know this couple. Please give me a word of wisdom; give me a word of knowledge, or some sort of insight, some sort of ability whereby I can minister effectively to this couple."

And the Bible says He'll give you as much as you need. Thank God that we have a generous God, that when we learn to beg, we will never, ever, ever drain His resources. He always has an ample supply, an ample supply of wisdom, of insight, of understanding. Whatever it is, power, authority, whatever you need at any given time, God has it.

God Chooses Weak People

Jesus is teaching us the necessity of dependency, the recognition that we are incapable of doing anything by ourselves. In First Corinthians 1:26-29, Paul writes:

> *Consider your calling, brethren, that there were not many wise according to the flesh, not many mighty, not many noble; but God has chosen the foolish things of the world to shame the wise, and God has chosen the weak things of the world to shame the things which are strong, and the base things of the world and the despised God has chosen, the things that are not, so that He may nullify the things that are, so that no man may boast before God.*

You see, God specializes in choosing weak individuals, things that are not, the foolish things, things that appear to be foolish in the natural. God purposely chooses those individuals for one reason: because they recognize their weakness. They recognize their inability, and therefore they have to depend totally upon God. Why doesn't He choose wise men, "not many wise" men? Because they are so full of their own wisdom, their own strength, their own ability, that God does not receive the glory. God rarely chooses those men so *"that no man may boast before God"* (1 Cor. 1:29).

That's why Paul said, *"When I am weak then I am strong"* (2 Cor. 12:10). The Lord said that His *"strength is made perfect in weakness"* (2 Cor. 12:9 NKJV). And so God will strip us. God will bring us to this place of weakness. Somewhere in your life He will strip you, just like He did with Moses. The Bible implies that when God first began to stir Moses' heart, he understood the call of God. It said, *"And he [Moses] supposed that his brethren understood that God was granting them deliverance through him, but they did not understand"* (Acts 7:25). In other words, he thought it was evident to everybody: "Look, I'm the man for the job." I believe that was the beginning of God's call upon his life.

However, before God could use him, He had to first strip him of his self-sufficiency. In order to do this, God arranges a way to send Moses to the back side of the desert. Why? Because Moses was operating in his own strength. The Bible says he was mighty in word and deed; he was powerful; he was eloquent; he was a son of Pharaoh's daughter; he was a king's kid; he had tutors; he went to the best school; he was gifted and bright, trained in all the ways of Egypt—and that was the problem that God had with him.

You see, one day Moses saw an Egyptian beating up one of the Israelites. Moses intervenes and kills the man, then buries him in the sand. Now imagine how long it would take to deliver the nation of Israel that way? You figure, one every day…basically, Moses would *still* be digging graves. God had a better idea, but He had to take Moses on the back side of the desert for 40 years. Finally God appears to him, but this time we see a very different Moses. Now we see a man stripped of his own self-sufficiency, free at last from the "I can" attitude of pride and arrogance.

God speaks to Moses, "Moses, I want you to go to Pharaoh."

"No, not me, I can't talk anymore. I sound like the sheep I've been around for the last 40 years. You know I stu-stut-stutter."

God says, "Now I can use you."

Moses has finally been brought to a place of total dependency. Notice his attitude: "Lord, who should I say sent me?" This is a far cry from supposing that his brethren understood that God had raised *him* up….

God answers Moses by saying, "Tell them 'I Am' has sent you." The word translated as "I Am" means: " I Am becoming _____," according to Rotherham's Emphasized translation. In other words, God is telling Moses that whatever he needs, God will become. "I am your wisdom. I am your peace. I am your provision. I am your strength. I am your righteousness. I am _____."

Just fill in the blank. I'm convinced that God will ultimately bring every man or woman of God to that place of utter dependency upon Him.

Heroes—Cream of the Crop or Average Joes?

One of my favorite portions of Scripture is in Hebrews chapter 11:

> *What more shall I say? For time will fail me if I tell of Gideon, Barak, Samson, Jephthah, of David and Samuel and the prophets, who by faith conquered kingdoms, performed acts of righteousness, obtained promises, shut the mouths of lions, quenched the power of fire, escaped the edge of the sword...became mighty in war, put foreign armies to flight* (Hebrews 11:32-34).

Now I think you would agree that's a pretty impressive list. After all, these are what we call the "heroes of faith." For many, many years I looked at those men and thought, *These are a breed all of their own. These men are unique, gifted, one in a million, so to speak. These are God's special agents, the equivalent of our Green Berets or Navy Seals.* I put them on a pedestal, out of reach for the common man. I could never be like them, so why try. These are the type of men that appear once in a lifetime. I mean, after all, look at them! When was the last time you conquered a kingdom? When was the last time you shut the mouth of a lion, quenched the power of fire, became mighty in war, and put foreign armies to flight? Not too many of us can testify to something of that magnitude.

If you're familiar with this passage of Scripture then you know that I left out one little phrase that changes everything—my favorite phrase, I think, in the whole Bible. Let's read that passage again with the phrase back in, and you'll notice how it turns the whole thing around. This is Hebrews 11:32-34 in its entirety:

> *What more shall I say? For time will fail me if I tell of Gideon, Barak, Samson, Jephthah, of David and Samuel and the prophets, who by faith conquered kingdoms, performed acts of righteousness, obtained promises, shut the mouths of lions, quenched the power of fire, escaped the edge of the sword, **from weakness were made strong**, became mighty in war, put foreign armies to flight.*

That one little phrase, "from weakness were made strong," describes every single one of those individuals. They all had the same common denominator: They were *weak*, ordinary, average individuals just like you and me. You see, God said, *"Not many wise"* men (1 Cor. 1:26). God purposely chooses the weak, the base, and the foolish. These were weak individuals. Let's go through the list.

Gideon

First you have Gideon. Most of you probably know the story of Gideon. The Midianites had come into the land of Israel and had destroyed everything. The children of Israel were hiding in caves, fearful of the Midianites. We are introduced to Gideon as he is threshing his wheat in the winepress. This was not the time for grapes—or else the grapes had been stripped from the vines by the Midianites—but there he is with his grain, threshing it. Perhaps like the widow woman who fed Elijah, Gideon is preparing to make a loaf of bread to eat before he died; I don't know.

Suddenly the angel of the Lord appears to him and says, "Gideon, you are a mighty man of valor" (see Judg. 6:12). I am sure that if we had the whole dialogue recorded, Gideon would have said, "Listen, quit joking with me. You've got the wrong

Gideon. Don't you know that there are 12 tribes in Israel. Some of the tribes are great tribes, like the tribe of Judah and the tribe of Levi. But I am from Manasseh, the least of all the tribes. Not only that, but my father's house is the least of all the families that make up our tribe. And, in my family, I am the least, the youngest. In other words, God, You've reached right down to the bottom of the barrel—to me" (see Judg. 6:15).

The Lord said, *"Go in this your strength"* (Judg. 6:14). What was Gideon's strength? It was the realization that he was nothing—just an earthen vessel. "Lord, I am not sufficient for this task. I cannot do it."

God basically says, "Good. Then you are the sort of person I'm looking for."

You see, the biggest problem with using humans to do God's will is trying to ensure that God gets the glory—not us. God will share everything with us except His glory. His love, His patience, His kindness, His longsuffering, His righteousness, His peace, His joy, His grace, His mercy... God freely gives us all those things, but He says, "My glory I will not share with any other" (see Isa. 42:8; 48:11).

When people perceive themselves as self-sufficient, they glory in their own wisdom. They glory in their own strength, their own ability. They brag about what they've done, like Nebuchadnezzar who walked around the wall of Babylon and said, "Look what I've done, this great city... Look, I mean, I'm responsible for all these incredible buildings, these hanging gardens (one of the seven wonders of the world). I am responsible; look what I've done." He was so full of himself that God had to remove him from his prestigious palace to a nearby pasture where he grew feathers like an eagle and chewed grass like a cow.

God told Nebuchadnezzar that he would remain in that animal-like condition, *"...until you recognize that the Most High is ruler over the realm of mankind and bestows it on whomever He wishes"* (Dan. 4:25). God is jealous of His glory, and so He chooses weak individuals who reflect back the glory to God Himself.

Barak

The next person in the list of heroes in Hebrews 11 is Barak. Barak, as you may recall, was the head of the Israelite army. He was the Ariel Sharon of his day, the Norman Schwarzkopf or Arnold Schwarzenegger of his time, and yet this mighty military man in charge of all the troops of Israel, was not willing to go out to battle unless a woman would go with him.

Now please don't accuse me of being anti-women. I thank God for every woman—without you we would not be here and you contribute so much to our world—but when it comes to fighting, most men don't require the help of a woman. Imagine you're a guy in the playground at school and somebody is beating up on you. Here you are, a young man, with everyone watching you. Your very manhood is at stake. So what do you do? Do you run and grab your little sister and say, "Sister, help me, help me!" I mean, that would be the height of humiliation, wouldn't it? What a declaration of weakness that you can't handle this yourself; you need your little sister to help you.

Barak basically said, "I will not go out to fight unless a lady goes with me" (see Judg. 4:8). Of course we know that woman to be none other than Deborah, a prophetess and Judge. Really, in all honesty, I can't blame Barak for wanting to have the wisest person he knew—the God-appointed Judge of Israel—along with him when he went up against a seemingly more powerful enemy. Yet the request makes him seem a little less "manly" than most of us would expect a typical military leader to be. But this awareness of his own inadequacy makes Barak the obvious God-choice.

Samson

Next we have Samson. Now, some of you might be thinking, "Well, this is obviously a misprint. Samson is the last one who should be in a lineup like this—a list of weak people whom God used." After all, to most people Samson is the very epitome of strength. We certainly never equate Samson with weakness.

"From weakness were made strong" (Heb. 11:34). Yes, even Samson. You see, we have a very distorted image of this man. Let me explain what I mean.

I was raised in church and, like most kids in Sunday school, I used to have a little children's Bible. It had quite a few pictures in it, and I distinctly remember one of Samson. He was pictured as though he had just won some major bodybuilder contest—the strongest man in the world type of guy, pushing down these great pillars. Every muscle in his body perfectly shaped and honed. But that wasn't the way he was at all.

I remember many times my father sharing his thoughts on this very passage. "When we get to Heaven," he said, "there will be all these lines, people wanting autographs. You'll see a line and say, 'Who is that for? ...Oh *Moses*, oh boy, better get his autograph. Who is this line for? ...The apostle Paul, wow, I'd like to meet him. And who is this for? ...Jeremiah, oh I'd love to meet Jeremiah. And what about this? ...Oh I'd like to meet John; you know, all that revelation that he had. So who is this line for? ...Samson? Really? That's Samson, oh wow.'"

"You'll look down the line and see a little scrawny runt of a guy, signing autographs, and say, 'No, you've made a mistake that can't be Samson.'"

You see, that was what was such a puzzlement to Delilah; she couldn't figure out his strength. Now imagine if she had cradled her head between his 52-inch chest, and his 24-inch biceps, and then asked, "How come you're so strong?" What a crazy question. Here is a man with arms like tree trunks and a chest like a barrel and she says, "How come you're so strong—what's your secret?"

But you see, Delilah's dilemma was that she couldn't figure this man out. He appeared to be no different from every other man she had ever met—apart from his incredible strength. And he said, "If you cut my hair, I will become weak like other men." His natural strength had nothing to do with his ability to wreak havoc on the Philistines. His strength came from his anointing and was derived from his relationship with God, *from weakness he was made strong.*

Jephthah

Following Samson we have Jephthah. Talk about the odds being stacked against you. I think Jephthah was possibly the most rejected man in the Bible, apart from Jesus Christ—who was, as we know, *"despised and rejected by men"* (Isa. 53:3 NKJV). But Jephthah comes a close second. He was a bastard, illegitimate. Can you imagine, an illegitimate child in the Old Testament? I mean, talk about a blight on your character; talk about having a stigma that you grow up with. Everybody in town knew that he was a bastard or illegitimate. The Bible says that he was rejected by his brethren and by all the elders of Gilead. In other words, his town turned against him. Yet God puts His anointing upon Jephthah and raises him up, and he becomes one of the judges of Israel. Talk about going from weakness to strength. What a beautiful and powerful illustration of God's grace. He lifts the beggar from the dunghill and makes him a prince with God.

David

David also makes the list of "weaklings" in Hebrews 11. We think we know David so well, don't we, but let's go back prior to his fame. As a young man, David looked after his father Jesse's sheep. He had no idea that while others never gave him a passing glance, God was watching his every move—and liked what He saw.

Saul was the king of Israel at this time, but due to his disobedience and rebellion God had determined to replace him with a man of His choosing. Following God's instructions, Samuel the Prophet goes to David's hometown, Bethlehem, to appoint a successor to King Saul.

Samuel, fearful of King Saul finding out what he is doing, tells the township of Bethlehem that he has come to offer sacrifices to the Lord. He makes a point of inviting David's father, Jesse, telling him to bring along his sons—eight in all. Jesse arranges to have only seven of his sons present, assuming that Samuel would have no interest in his youngest son David.

Imagine how you would feel if some great man of God invited your family to some special event—one of those days that you would never forget as long as you live—and yet you are not even told about it, let alone invited.

I can picture the family getting ready, wondering what to wear and how to act in the presence of this "national hero." Following the sacrifice, Jesse presents his boys to Samuel. Samuel is quickly drawn to Eliab and immediately assumes he is the man for the job. God tells Samuel he is not impressed with outward appearance but with the condition of man's heart (see 1 Sam. 16:7). Soon all seven sons are eliminated.

I can just picture Samuel looking somewhat puzzled, as he turns to Jesse and says, "Have I made a mistake? Is this everyone? I thought you had your whole family here?"

And I can see Jesse's head dropping in embarrassment, as he answers, "There's one more." Or, in the precise words of the Bible, *"There remains yet the youngest"* (1 Sam. 16:11). In the Hebrew that word means "the least," not just numerically, but in every sense of the word. Basically, Jesse is saying "Has it come to this? David?"

Some of the Orthodox Jews believe that David was illegitimate because in Psalm 51:5, a psalm attributed to David, it says, *"In sin my mother conceived me."* Regardless of whether that is truly the case, there was something about David that kept him apart from the rest of the family. He was sort of a reject. And now we know the rest of the story. "From weakness he was made strong."

I believe the key to David's life is found in the phrase: "David inquired of the Lord... David inquired of the Lord...David inquired of the Lord." Time, after time, we see David not knowing what action to take and so he casts himself upon the Lord for His counsel and direction. DEPENDENCY—that's why David was so great. He didn't use his own wisdom; he didn't use his own expertise, his own ability, his own charisma. Instead David sought the mind of the Lord, "Should I do this? Should I go war against the Philistines? Should I..."

Samuel

Finally we have Samuel. Samuel was a young boy in the temple. The Bible says, *"Word from the Lord was rare in those days"* (1 Sam. 3:1). There was no message, no prophet; nobody was really hearing from God. There was a famine of hearing the Word of God. And then God reached down to the life of a young boy— bypassing Eli and his sons, Hophni and Phinehas, the spiritual leaders of the day who were not living right before God—and He reaches down and whispers into the ear of a little boy. All of a sudden the ears of everyone in Israel are tingling with the news that God is appearing and speaking to the boy Samuel. What a beautiful picture of weakness turned to strength.

Now It's Our Turn

I share this study of weak "heroes" with you because I know that some of you have already written yourself off. You've believed a lie of the enemy that God could never use someone like you. You've used the excuses: "I don't have a good education"; "I don't have much of a personality"; "I have some skeletons in the closet"; "If people only knew about my past...." You've bought into the belief that God could never use you. But I'm here to tell you, God specializes in taking weak individuals, cleansing those individuals, bringing them to that place of dependency, and then placing His anointing and His authority upon their life.

I went to a small Bible school—we had about 35 students in our class—and every few weeks the students would go out on ministry trips. They were asked to go out and testify or to sing or speak. In the three years that I attended that school, I was never once asked to go on a single trip. Now I could understand why I was never asked to sing. That was obvious to anyone who listened to me. And looking back I can see why I was never called upon to minister in any way. I was incredibly shy, incredibly nervous, incredibly introspective. I could never speak publicly. My head used to shake if ever I was asked to speak. It's one thing when your knees knock together, but my head would shake uncontrollably the more self-conscious I became. It was indescribably terrifying for me for years, something that I had to cry out to God to overcome. I know what it is honestly to go from weakness to strength.

There are hundreds of times when I've gotten down on my face before God, in my own devotional times, and wept like a baby and said, "God, I cannot believe I'm doing what I'm doing as I look back at what I used to be." I say that to encourage you. Three years in Bible school and I was never chosen. Why? Because man looks at the outward appearance. We go by charisma; we go by personality; we go by natural strength and intellect. God, however, doesn't really care about any of that. God chooses the weak, the foolish, base, and despised.

Be Strong in the Lord

God's Word exhorts us to *"be strong in the Lord and in the strength of His might"* (Eph. 6:10).

As a little boy living in England, I went to a school about a mile away from our house. On the way home from school I often passed some other students making their way home from another school. Some of these students would surround me on the street and rough me up a little bit. Here I was, a little English boy wearing my gray flannel shorts with my satchel or leather bag on my back. I used to dread seeing these other students because they were usually in an upbeat mood. If they caught sight of me, they would chase me, throw rocks, or whatever, and if they could grab me and rough me up a little bit, they would. I would watch out for them, and if I could see them coming, I'd go down some back alley and make it home some other way.

But occasionally my father would come to school and pick me up and we would walk home together. As we walked I could see those same kids, and I could thumb my nose, you know, do all sorts of things, without fear—despite the fact that I was no different than I was the day before. I was no stronger. I hadn't taken a course in self-defense or pumped iron all night. I was still as weak and as puny as I was the day before. But you see, I was now strong in my father's strength. "Be strong in the Lord and in the strength of His might."

My might was no different, but I had a relationship; I had somebody with me. We've got to learn this place of dependency where we can say, "God, I am totally and completely dependent upon You." The Bible says that *we have this treasure in earthen vessels* (2 Cor. 4:7). We've got to recognize our earthen vessel; it's nothing, yet we have the grace and the power of God available to us.

God Wants Empty Vessels

Let me take you to one other story found in Second Kings chapter 4. Here we have the tragic story of a woman whose husband dies. The Bible says that her husband was considered one of the *sons of the prophets* (2 Kings 4:1). In that same verse, she comes to another prophet, Elisha, and says, "Your servant my husband is dead, and you know that your servant feared the Lord; and the creditor has come to take my two children to be his slaves."

Apparently due to her husband's death, she had accumulated lots of debt that she had no way of paying, and the creditors had come to take her two kids. We don't know how old her children were, but no doubt they were old enough to be sold as slaves.

This poor woman has not only gone through the trauma of losing her husband, but now she's faced with the added trauma of having her children taken from her, maybe seeing them put up for auction, being sent away to some distant land or something. She's faced with the possibility of never seeing them again, and so she's crying out to the prophet for help.

The prophet says to her, "Well, what do you have in your house?" Oh, maybe he'd been in the house many times when the former prophet was there, and the two of them had formed a friendship. Perhaps he recalls the last time he was in the house and remembers some of the items. If we were to modernize the story, it would go something like this:

"Last time I was here you had a beautiful grand piano. Why don't you sell it? That would certainly tide you over for a little while, pay off some of your debts."

"Oh the piano went months ago."

"Well, I don't know. You had a riding mower. What about that?"

"Yes, but we got rid of that too."

"How about that beautiful antique bedroom set you had?"

"We've already sold it."

"What about that big double-wide refrigerator?"

"That's gone too."

"Then what do you have in the house? You've got to have something that you can sell."

"Listen, I've told you. We've sold everything. We don't have a single thing of value left except this little jar of oil."

"I'll tell you what to do," says the prophet. "Go and borrow as many empty vessels as you can get your hands on. Once you've done that, go into your house and shut the door. Then take that little jar of oil and begin to fill those empty vessels."

Here we have one of the most powerful illustrations of dependency. I heard a man of God once say: *The more emptiness you can present to God, the more of His fullness you can receive.*

You see, the biggest problem with most of us is that we're already full—full of our own strength, our own ability, our own wisdom, our own insight, our own giftedness—which means there is very little room left for God. Is it any wonder then that God chooses weak, base, empty vessels, because then He can pour in His life. That's why if we do consider ourselves up to the task, God will strip and empty us out, so to speak, and drain us of our own resources. It may not happen for a few years. We may be able to "wing it" for a little while, but somewhere down the line, if we really follow God, He will bring us to that place where He strips us totally and completely of every capability in the natural, so that He can fill us with all the resources of Heaven. *"Blessed are the [beggars], for theirs is the kingdom of Heaven"* (Matt. 5:3).

You might think I'm belaboring this point, but it is essential that we embrace it as a principle upon which to build our lives. Jesus said, *"I am come that you might have life"* (see John 10:10). In other words, we constantly need to recognize our utter dependency upon Him and Him alone.

Dr. Martyn-Lloyd Jones, in his exposition of the Sermon on the Mount, says of being "poor in spirit":

It is the fundamental characteristic of the Christian and of the citizen of the kingdom of Heaven, and all other characteristics are in a sense a result of this one. As we go on to expound it, we shall see that it really means an emptying, while the others are a manifestation of fullness. We cannot be filled until we are empty.

He goes on to say:

It means a complete absence of pride, a complete absence of self-assurance and of self-reliance. It means a consciousness that we are nothing in the presence of God. It is nothing then that we

*can produce; it is nothing that we can do in ourselves. It is just this tremendous awareness of our utter nothingness as we come face to face with God. That is to be "poor in spirit." Let me put it as strongly as I can, and I do so on the basis of the teaching of the Bible. It means this, that if we are truly Christian we shall not rely upon our natural birth. We shall not rely upon the fact that we belong to certain families; we shall not boast that we belong to certain nations or nationalities. We shall not build upon our natural temperament. We shall not believe in and rely upon our natural position in life, or any powers that may have been given to us. We shall not rely upon money or any wealth we may have. The thing about which we may boast will not be the education or the particular school or college to which we have been. No, all that is to what Paul came to regard as "dung" and a hindrance to this greater thing because it tended to master and control him. We shall not rely upon any gifts like that of natural "personality," or intelligence or general or special ability. We shall not rely upon our own morality and conduct and good behavior. We shall not bank to the slightest extent on the life we have lived or are trying to live. No; we shall regard all that as Paul regarded it. That is "poverty of spirit."
...I say again, it is to feel that we are nothing, and that we have nothing, and that we look to God in utter submission to Him and in utter dependence upon Him and His grace and mercy.*[1]

Oswald Chambers writes in his book, *Studies in the Sermon on the Mount*:

The Sermon on the Mount will produce despair in the heart of the natural man; and that is the very thing Jesus means it to do, because immediately we reach the point of despair we are willing to come to Jesus as paupers and to receive from Him. "Blessed are the poor in spirit"—that is the first principle of the kingdom. As long as we have a conceited, self-righteous idea that we can do the thing if God will help us, God has to allow us to go on until we break the neck of our ignorance over some obstacle then we will be willing to come and receive from Him. The bedrock of Jesus Christ's Kingdom is poverty, not possession; not decisions for Jesus Christ, but a sense of absolute futility—I cannot begin to do it. Then says Jesus, "Blessed are you."[2]

In Song of Solomon, we see the bride coming up out of the desert, or wilderness, leaning on her beloved. That's how God wants the Church to be, leaning on Him. There's a song we used to sing many years ago that said, "Leaning on the everlasting arms, I'm leaning, leaning...." That's the place of dependency. We're no longer self-sufficient, or self-reliant, but we're leaning; we're absolutely and totally dependent upon the Lord Jesus Christ for everything.

I've spent a great deal of time on this first principle because it is vital that we understand its importance. It's the most critical one; everything else hinges upon it. I look at my own life and at the life of others, and I'm convinced that this is the key to longevity in ministry. The moment you begin to draw from your own strength, your own resources, your own ability, that very moment we are sending God a clear message that He is no longer needed and that we can handle things alone.

Uzziah in the Old Testament is a perfect example of this. We are told that *"As long as he sought the Lord, God prospered him"* (2 Chron. 26:5). Here we see a man who knew what it was to seek the face of God for everything. His time alone with God was evident to all—God caused him to prosper. But then the Bible says, "When he became strong" God forsook him (see 2 Chron. 26:15-21). Nothing is more tragic than to have God withdraw His hand of blessing from your life.

God wants to pour His Spirit into us, but we have to be empty. We've got to recognize our need. "Lord, I don't have it, but You do…. Lord, here is my cup, fill it up." That should be our prayer. If you're one of those people who are working in your own strength, your own ability, say, "Lord, just empty me. Lord, I am tired of trying to do it my way; I want to learn to do it Your way. I want to be like the pattern Son, the Lord Jesus Christ, who could do nothing of Himself, who didn't initiate a single thing. And Lord, I want to humbly accept and proclaim the statement of Jesus in John 15:5, *'Apart from Me you can do* [absolutely] *nothing.'"*

Please pray with me. "Father, I thank You that You delight in taking weak, empty vessels, so that You can pour Your life into them, Your strength into them, Your wisdom into them, and Your anointing into their lives. Help us to recognize, Lord, that we don't have any strength, we don't have any ability apart from Your grace. Lord, keep us in that place of dependency. Lord, don't ever let us get to a place where we become independent. Father, destroy that independence that is within every single one of us. Lord, keep us on our face before You, in Jesus' name, amen."

Endnotes

1. David Martyn-Lloyd Jones, *Studies in the Sermon on the Mount* (Grand Rapids, MI: Eerdmans Publishing, 1984), 42, 50.

2. Oswald Chambers, *Studies in the Sermon on the Mount* (London: Simpkin Marshall, Ltd., 1932), 12.

Chapter 2

Intimacy

Have you ever thought what a wonderful privilege it is that everyone each day and each hour of the day has the liberty of asking God, to meet Him in the inner chamber, and to hear what He has to say? ...Christ came from Heaven to love us with the love wherewith the Father loved Him. He suffered and died to win our hearts for this love. His love can be satisfied with nothing less than a deep, personal love on our part.

—Andrew Murray

THE anointing of the Spirit of God is that divine enabling that transcends man's natural ability and intellect and equips them for the task to which God has called them. John reminds us in his Epistle that *"the anointing which you received from Him abides in you"* (1 John 2:27). This very precious enduement of the Holy Spirit is not to be taken for granted or treated lightly. It is vital that we understand the necessity of "guarding" that which has been entrusted to us. The Spirit of God is easily grieved or quenched;

therefore we are looking at some of the principles that ensure us longevity and continued effectiveness in our calling and ministry.

I carry in my Bible a statement by John Maxwell. John Maxwell is well recognized in leadership circles as a spiritual mentor and father figure. In his book, *The Twenty-One Most Powerful Minutes in a Leader's Day*, he states: "Only one person out of every ten who enters the ministry will still be in it when he reaches the age of 65." Those are documented statistics; they're not mine. One person out of ten who enters the ministry will still be ministering at the age of 65. Something needs to be done to stem this spiritual hemorrhaging in the Body of Christ.

Human Resources Are Not Enough

In the first chapter we began by looking at Jesus as the "pattern Son." Peter exhorts us to *"follow in His steps"* (1 Pet. 2:21). The first principle that we looked at was this whole area of dependency. Jesus said He could do nothing of Himself. We find that principle all the way through the Word of God—dependency upon the Lord. There are so many stories that serve to illustrate this point. Take for example Jesus looking at the 5,000 people who had followed Him because of the signs and wonders He was performing. Jesus was aware of their natural hunger and He turns to His disciples and says, *"You give them something to eat"* (Luke 9:13). What a far cry that is from those in ministry today who rely upon the crowds to feed their needs. How times have changed.

The disciples apparently have no food to feed anyone with, nor do they have enough money to buy food for all the people. But then Andrew finds a young boy with a few loaves and fish— which then raises the question, *"But what are they* [the loaves and fish] *among so many?"* (John 6:9). Jesus had obviously set up this situation, wishing to prove to them that His *"strength is made perfect in* [our] *weakness"* (2 Cor. 12:9 NKJV).

Most of us have heard the saying: Man's extremity is God's opportunity. Well, imagine if you just had two little sardines and a few small hamburger buns to feed 5,000 hungry men plus the women and children. I don't think anybody would really get satisfied with that. It would barely provide a single crumb per person. However, when the little bit that we have is placed into the hands of the Master, when He begins to get a hold of it and begins the breaking process, the end result is that the needs of the multitudes are adequately met. The end of that portion of Scripture says that *"they all ate and were satisfied"* (Luke 9:17).

In other words, it wasn't just a little appetizer that took the edge off their hunger for a while, but it was something that totally filled them to the point of being satisfied. Only God can do that. God can take our inadequacies and shortcomings and exchange them for His sufficiency.

We have another wonderful story in the Book of Exodus, where the children of Israel face their first conflict after coming out of Egypt. (See Exodus 17.) They meet up with the Amalekites, who swoop down on the Israelites, and there is a battle. It's the very first battle that the children of Israel encounter after their "conversion"; they've been redeemed by the blood of the lamb. And it isn't too long after you're born again by the Spirit of God that the enemy comes to try to get back everything that has been taken from him, and so he swoops down like the Amalekites. The Amalekites are called *"the sinners, the Amalekites"* (1 Sam. 15:18); that's the definition the Bible gives to the Amalekites, "the sinners." Sin is always seeking a way to gain access into our lives and take dominion.

In the midst of the battle, Moses sent Joshua down to fight against the Amalekites. In the meantime, Moses stations himself on top of a nearby mountain—not to escape the battle, but to pray. As he is wrestling in prayer, his arms uplifted before God, he becomes tired and his hands begin to droop. The Bible says that as long as Moses' hands are raised, Joshua is able to overwhelm the Amalekites; however, when Moses· lets his hands down, Amalek prevails (see Exod. 17:11). The key then to Joshua's success was the fact that Moses was praying and crying out to God on behalf of Israel.

As that day goes on, Moses' energy begins to fail, giving the Amalekites the advantage. Aaron and Hur perceive what is going on and move in to support the hands of Moses. As they raise his hands up, one standing on one side, one standing on the other, Joshua is able to defeat the Amalekites. In the margin of the New International Version of the Bible, there is an alternate translation of Exodus 17:16, which says: *"Because a hand was against the throne of the Lord."* In other words, when Moses had his hands raised, he was making contact with the throne of God. And as long as you and I have contact with the throne of God, we will be successful in living a holy and purposeful life. We cannot defeat sin or defeat the enemy in our own strength or our own ability, but as long as you and I maintain contact with the throne of God, all things are possible. He alone causes us to triumph.

You and I have to constantly come into the presence of God. We were never designed to be self-sufficient. God never created us to be self-sufficient. He created us to rely on Him for everything.

The Importance of Intimacy With God

We now come to the next principle—that of intimacy. If we understand dependency correctly, it will drive us to intimacy. In other words, using the illustration of Luke 11, it is only when we recognize that we have no bread that we will go to the source that does have bread. The unprepared host (discussed in the previous chapter) who wanted to satisfy the needs of his friend came to the realization that he had absolutely nothing to set before him. This in turn led him to the one (his neighbor) who had an abundance. In the same way, dependency upon God should drive us to this place of intimacy with God Himself.

Jesus said in John 14:10, *"The Father abiding in Me does His works."* In other words, Jesus maintained an intimate relationship with the Father. He had an abiding relationship. He didn't run to the Father every once in a while; rather, it was a constant relationship that He had with Him. Jesus was showing His disciples that intimacy with the Father was the key to everything He did.

We see Jesus stressing this when He says, *"If you abide in Me, and My words abide in you, ask whatever you wish, and it will be done for you"* (John 15:7). "If you abide"—this whole area of abiding is so absolutely essential in the Christian life. We must maintain intimacy with God on a daily, hourly, moment by moment basis. John 15 is a very wonderful chapter, and yet in that chapter Jesus never really defines abiding. He simply says that we need to abide: *"Abide in Me, and I in you"* (John 15:4).

That same verse goes on to say, *"As the branch cannot bear fruit of itself unless it abides in the vine, so neither can you unless you abide in Me."* You and I cannot produce the fruit that God is looking for in and of ourselves, unless we abide in Him. And so He tells us here to be in this place of constant abiding.

In the following chapter of John's Gospel, Jesus continues with, *"These things I have spoken to you that you may be kept from stumbling"* (John 16:1). What were the "things" He was referring to? Chapter 15. In other words, the thing that keeps us from falling, the thing that keeps us from stumbling, is to abide. Jesus is basically saying, "I have taught you about abiding because it will keep you from stumbling; it will keep you from falling."

John Stressed the Importance of "Abiding"

John expounds the principle of abiding in his Epistle. In his Gospel he exhorts us to abide, but if we go into his Epistle we find that not only is he still stressing the vital importance of abiding, but he begins to explain in more detail exactly what he means by abiding. For instance, he shows that we can have *"fellowship...with the Father, and with His Son Jesus Christ"* (1 John 1:3). So here again we find this place of intimacy. John then shows how this place of fellowship or intimacy is conditional upon walking in the light or truthfulness. He reminds us that *"God is Light, and in Him there is no darkness at all. If we say that we have fellowship with Him and yet walk in the darkness, we lie and do not practice the truth"* (1 John 1:5-6). So if we say that we abide, if we say that we have intimacy, if we say that we have fellowship and yet we walk in darkness, we are really deceiving ourselves.

One of the keys to abiding is walking in the light, walking in openness, walking in transparency, walking in honesty before God. As long as we maintain that transparency, that honesty, that openness, then we can abide in fellowship with Him. John continues to challenge those who say *"I have come to know Him"* yet do not keep His commandments (1 John 2:4). John declares them to be "liars" having no truth in them. He further says that the one who *"keeps His Word, in him the love of God has truly been perfected"*; thereby proving that we are *"in Him"* (1 John 2:5).

If we want to abide, if we want to be in Him, then the Bible says we have to keep His Word. In other words, obedience is one of the keys to abiding. If we want to know Him, we have to walk in obedience.

John continues by saying, *"The one who says he abides in Him ought himself to walk in the same manner as He walked"* (1 John 2:6). Another key to abiding is to walk in the same manner as Jesus walked. Now that has nothing to do with the way in which He walked in the natural; the "walk" that John is referring to is Jesus' whole life—from His conversation to His conduct. I think it was A.W. Tozer who said, "If you want to grow spiritually, you need to love what God loves and hate what God hates." If you truly want to abide in Him, learn to love what God loves, learn to hate what God hates; that's what it means to walk even as He walked.

John seems determined to show us the full spectrum of what abiding means. He continues on with, *"The one who loves his brother abides in the Light and there is no cause for stumbling"* (1 John 2:10). To abide in the light—what or who is the light? The obvious reference is to the Lord Jesus Christ. We cannot abide unless we love one another. Why? Because *"God is love"* (1 John 4:8). *"What fellowship has light with darkness?"* (2 Cor. 6:14).

In other words, if we're not in agreement, if we're not keeping His commandments, if we're not walking the way He walked, then we cannot have a true relationship; we cannot have real fellowship with Him. Two cannot walk together unless they are in agreement.

John seems to be stressing even more the importance of abiding as he continues to challenge those who seemingly rather flippantly regard themselves as "spiritual" or "doing OK." He warns them, *"Do not love the world nor the things in the world. If anyone loves the world, the love of the Father is not in him"* (1 John 2:15). Here again he stresses that there can be no genuine relationship—fellowship, abiding—if we are still deeply attracted and attached to the world. John makes clear that to love the world is to be at enmity with God—as we also learn from James: *"Friendship with the world is enmity with God"* (James 4:4 NKJV). Being friends with the world means that you are at war with God.

Fellowship with God requires separation from all else. There has to be that "first love" relationship, where Jesus Christ is more important to us than anything else in the world. David expressed it well when he wrote: *"Whom have I in heaven but You? And besides You, I desire nothing on earth"* (Ps. 73:25).

John continues this theme into chapter 3 of First John, *"No one who abides in Him sins; no one who sins has seen Him or knows Him"* (1 John 3:6). Again, we are given insight and understanding into the secret of abiding—not to practice sin. John clarifies this by saying that *"if anyone sins, we have an Advocate with the Father"* (1 John 2:1)—not *when* we sin.

If or When

I can recall my father, when I was a little boy, traveling to America. In those days it was cheaper to go by ship than it was to fly, and so he would travel on the Queen Elizabeth or the Queen Mary, both of which have now been retired from service.

The transatlantic crossing would take seven days from Southampton to New York. My father would explain that within a matter of hours of the ship's leaving port they would sound an alarm to gather everyone on deck. Every passenger was required to bring with them their life jacket—they were about to undergo a "lifeboat drill."

The instructor would thoroughly brief the assembled passengers, instructing them how to put on and secure their life jackets in case of trouble. "If there is a fire onboard or some other emergency, you need to know this information." He would tell them what to do.

My father said that the instructor always used the words: *"if the boat goes down."* If he had phrased it, *"when the boat goes down,"* my father said he would have shouted, "Back up and let me off." *When* assumes that it is going down; however, *if* suggests there is a good possibility that nothing will happen. The Bible says, *"If anyone sins, we have an Advocate with the Father"* (see 1 John 2:1), not when we sin.

You have an eraser on the end of a pencil in case you make a mistake, that is, *if* you make a mistake. You don't purposely mis-spell words in order to use the eraser. Neither is that what the blood of Jesus Christ is all about. We don't just continue on in sin and say, "Well, God is the divine eraser, and it doesn't matter what I do; I can go out and enjoy myself sexually or any other way and then at the end of the day I can just turn the pencil over, so to speak, and Jesus will forgive me." No! It's *if* we sin.

And so John says, *"Whoever abides in Him does not sin"* (1 John 3:6 NKJV). That is important.

John drills home this theme of abiding in First John 3:17, *"Whoever has the world's goods, and sees his brother in need and clos-es his heart against him, how does the love of God abide in him?"* Interesting, isn't it? In other words, if you see needs, and you have the capability of meeting those needs, and yet you refuse to take care of the needs of a brother, or sister, and so on, how does the love of God abide in you? How can you have that abiding rela-tionship? God who was rich, for our sake became poor and freely gave of Himself when He saw a need. Therefore if we are going to abide in Him, and know Him, and have this intimacy with Him, and walk the way He walked, then we have to practice what He practiced.

Finally, John declares, *"The one who keeps His commandments abides in Him, and He in him. We know by this that He abides in us, by the Spirit whom He has given us"* (1 John 3:24). The one who keeps His commandments abides in Him. These then are some of the insights that John reveals regarding this vitally important truth of abiding.

Jesus Stressed the Importance of Intimacy With God

Another powerful illustration of intimacy is revealed when Jesus appointed the 12 disciples. The Scripture states *"He appointed twelve, so that they would be with Him and that He could send them out to preach"* (Mark 3:14). I have a friend who says, "You have no right to go out to preach unless you spend time *with Him.*" In other words, intimacy with Jesus is essential if we are to be effective ministers. Jesus didn't appoint 12 men simply to be sent forth to minister; rather, first they were to be "with Him." This is the key to anointed preaching—this is the key to the Christian life.

I am very much indebted to two men who left a profound impact on my life. One was my father, who was a true man of prayer. Somebody asked me the other day, "What one teaching did your father leave you that you think of more than any other?"

And I had to say to them, "I don't think there was any particular teaching that my father left me, other than a life exemplified by godliness. There wasn't a particular message, no particular little phrase, but rather the observation of his life over the years that made the most profound impact." One of the things I observed my father doing on a daily basis was praying, sometimes four or five or six hours a day. He died when he was 87 years of age, yet he was still rising every single night consistently for two hours to pray, even at age 87. Most men are retired by then with little if any desire to pray.

The other gentleman who left a profound impact on my life was a man by the name of Peter Morrow. He's now gone to be with the Lord—a wonderful man of God. I had the privilege of working with him for 15 years in Christchurch, New Zealand. Peter used to spend most of his time in a little room no larger than a closet at the back of his bedroom where he would fast and pray.

The church Peter pastored steadily grew to be one of the largest churches in New Zealand with around 1,500 in attendance. Peter preferred to "office" out of his closet rather than the church itself. It was rare to find him in the building apart from meetings.

One thing I could always count on was that at least every few months my phone would ring and the church secretary would say, "Peter is on the line." I would pick up the phone and Brother Peter would say, "David, I'm coming into town this afternoon. How about going out for a milkshake?"

All six of the pastoral staff knew what having a milkshake with Peter meant. It meant that we were going to find a little coffee shop somewhere, sit down in a corner, and Peter would begin to question me as to how I was doing. It was a type of pastoral interrogation motivated by his desire to see others excel in their calling and ministry. He'd always ask about things like my marriage, "How are you and Nancy getting along?" And if I gave a sort of pat answer, he always knew it, and he'd say, "Come on, look at me, how are you really doing?" He was a master at unearthing information, but he did it in such a loving way that you knew you just couldn't hold anything back.

It was rare to spend this special time with Peter without him asking me about my prayer time. Repeatedly over the years he would say to me, "David, I don't ever want you coming into the office until I know you've spent an hour on your face before God." To him it didn't matter if I came in at lunchtime; it didn't matter if I stayed away all day, not that I ever did, as long as he knew I was in the presence of God. He understood this basic principle, "You have to be with Him before you go out to preach." To Peter, prayer was the number one priority of the ministry. He knew that all effective ministry is born from the place of prayer.

I have never forgotten those times. They instilled in me a discipline and desire that by the grace of God I have maintained ever since. Very seldom does a day go by that I don't get my hour alone with the Lord. I am indebted to Peter Morrow for that. When I pastored, I was always in my office by eight o'clock, normally about five or ten minutes early. I would slip into the office and immediately cover the window in my office door (which was there for "integrity" while counseling). I would then lock my door and let the church secretary know that she was not to disturb me until at least sometime after nine o'clock. So, between eight and nine o'clock, every single morning, without exception, I was on my face before God. That was the way my day began.

Intimacy with God is absolutely imperative. Jeremiah 9:23 says, *"Let not a wise man boast of his wisdom, and let not the mighty man boast of his might, let not a rich man boast about his riches"*; the next verse goes on to say that if you boast about anything, boast in this, that you know and understand the Lord. There's only one thing worth boasting about. It's not the size of your bank account; it's not your position or your rank in the world. Boast in one thing only, and that's your relationship with God. (Now I'm not suggesting that you make other Christians feel like your relationship with God is better than theirs; that's not what I mean by "boast." I'm simply pointing out that the only thing of value that we have is our relationship with God.) The only way possible to develop a relationship with somebody is to spend time with that individual.

You can take any three or four people, lock them in a room for 24 hours, deprive them of any communication other than their ability to talk to one another, and I guarantee that at the end of 24 hours they will be able to introduce one another, tell you where they grew up, when or if they married, had children, the type of job they have, the type of food they like etc., etc. Because all they've done for 24 hours is talk, talk, talk, talk, talk.

You increase that to 48 hours, or increase that to a week, or you put them on a desert island somewhere for two months, and you can guarantee that the more time they spend together the more they will become familiar with each other because they've had all that time just to sit there, with little else to do, other than communicate. The only way you ever get to know God is by spending time in His presence, spending time in the Word of God, and beginning to muse and meditate and seek God with all your heart. There is no other way; there is no shortcut. It would be tempting if there was, but there isn't.

The Book of Daniel says, *"The people who know their God shall be strong, and carry out great exploits"* (Dan. 11:32 NKJV)—those who *know* their God.

I wonder why we don't see great exploits? I think truthfully we don't know God. I was talking the other day with a friend about the incredible need for a breakthrough in the area of healing. We need to see some exploits; we need to see men and women set free from bondage, fear, sickness, and disease. Why don't we? Maybe it goes back to this: We really don't know God the way we should know Him. If we knew God, I believe we would see the exploits that we long to see.

In First Samuel 2:12, we are introduced to the leadership of Israel at the time when Samuel was just a little boy, and it says concerning the leaders, *"Now the sons of Eli were worthless men; they did not know the Lord."* What a tragedy. Here are two men, priests, set apart for the ministry, two of the main leaders of the nation of Israel—who are *supposed* to be the spiritual leaders of the nation of Israel—and yet the Bible makes it very, very clear that they were worthless men. They did not know the Lord.

How can you be a priest and not know God? Yet here they were. If you look at what they did, you realize they didn't know God. They misused and abused their spiritual authority. They were involved in immorality, greed, and other ungodly attitudes and actions—which is why the Bible calls them "worthless."

To avoid becoming "worthless" ourselves, we need to ask God, "Lord, put a desire, put a hunger, in me to know You." Paul said at the end of his life, *"that I may know Him"* (Phil. 3:10). Paul had been caught up to the third heaven; he'd had all sorts of revelations that we still don't know anything about because he was not allowed to even utter them. And yet, in spite of all of that, in spite of experiencing all sorts of signs and wonders and miracles, and so on, he still has this deep longing, "that I may know Him." It was a lifelong determination that Paul had; he was never fully satisfied, always hungering for more and more of God. God is so vast that we will never exhaust the resources of knowing Him. So daily we come and we seek to know Him.

Moses had this same intense longing. In Exodus 33:13 he said, *"Let me know Your ways* **that I may know You.**" Here we find Moses, who has seen all sorts of miracles. He had seen the Nile turn to blood at his command, as well as all the other plagues. He had watched the firstborn of Egypt destroyed, and later the entire army of Egypt destroyed in the Red Sea, not to mention the spectacular opening of the Red Sea. All of these things he had seen, and yet he still has this hunger to know more and more of God.

It doesn't matter what you've seen or experienced in the past; it's that deep longing, "Lord, I want more, and more, and more, and more of You." And if you don't have that, then ultimately you will not survive the anointing.

In Paul's first letter to Timothy, he writes, *"Pay close attention to yourself and to your teaching; persevere in these things, for as you do this you will ensure salvation both for yourself and for those who hear you"* (1 Tim. 4). Paul is not saying to Timothy, "Listen, play a little golf, make sure you find time for your daily afternoon nap...." No, he's talking about looking after himself spiritually. Paul is saying, "Timothy, pay attention to your own spiritual well-being, because if you don't, the church ultimately is going to suffer. But if you do, then you will ensure salvation, both for yourself and for those who listen to you." Paul's ultimate concern is for the well-being of the flock.

Paul states the same thing while talking to the elders of Ephesus in Acts 20:28, *"Be on guard for yourselves and for all the flock, among which the Holy Spirit has made you overseers."* Notice he puts the elders first, *"Be on guard* [first of all] *for yourself."* He's warning them about things that are about to happen. We need to guard our personal lives in order to protect the flock of God. This principle still holds true for every single one of us.

One of the first decisions the early Church had to make as they began to grow was in regard to the needs of the widows. The apostles were spending many, many hours preparing meals and serving tables. They were attempting to cater to the growing need of the widows. They soon came to the realization, however, that they were neglecting two very important things: God's Word and prayer. So they appointed deacons to take care of that particular facet of ministry, caring for the widows, and said, *"We will give ourselves continually to prayer and to the ministry of the Word"* (Acts 6:4 NKJV).

Tools for Intimacy: Word of God and Prayer

We cannot neglect those two very, very vital functions of the Christian life: the Word of God and prayer. It is the Word of God that makes us wise unto salvation; it's the Word of God that causes us to grow and develop. As newborn babes, desire the sincere milk of the Word that you may grow. We will never develop spiritually without the Word of God; we will never develop relationally without coming into fellowship and intimacy with God Himself.

About a year and a half ago I was driven to an airport in Michigan by an elderly man in his late 70s. The senior pastor where I had been ministering for that weekend had brought him out of retirement to be in charge of pastoral care and counseling. As we shared together he made the statement that he had never had to counsel a minister involved in sexual sin who had maintained his own personal devotional life. In other words, the "problem" begins long before the crisis comes, due to not feeding on the Word of God or spending time daily in His presence.

I believe it was Dr. Martyn Lloyd-Jones who said, "Good preaching eliminates the need for counseling." Now I don't know if I agree with that 100 percent, but I do believe there is an incredible amount of truth to it. If we get into the Word of God ourselves, it makes us wise unto salvation; it gives us insight and understanding and teaches us how to cope with life, how to handle the problems of life, and so on. When we neglect the Word of God, we neglect the Word of God to our own peril. I don't want to be legalistic here in any way, but I do believe that if we are healthy spiritually, we will want to partake of God's Word.

The only reason a baby will *not* take to the breast is because of some sort of sickness. A baby in the natural is hungry and *wants* to be fed. In the same way, we should want to draw the life of God into us; and if we do not, then there is something seriously wrong with our Christian life. Why don't I desire the sincere milk of the Word?

Again, I'm trying to emphasize this because it is the key to spiritual growth, the key to maintaining the anointing, the key to longevity in the Christian life. It ensures that you don't become a castaway, or simply "peter out" somewhere along the way.

True Love Finds the Time

Many Christians seem to have a legalistic relationship with God and His Word, which is one of bondage; the love relationship is one of freedom. When my wife and I were attending Bible college, we had only a small class of about 35 students. We began dating in our second year; and boy, we were deeply in love. Our greatest problem was that the school was extremely strict regarding its rules.

I was in my early 20s at the time. We were only allowed to go off campus once a month, for our day off. The only problem with that was you had to be back on campus by 10:30 at night. Not only that, but if you took a girl out, or you were a girl going out with a boy, you had to go to the dean of men's office (or the dean of women). Outside the office there was a book. You were required to write your name in the book, and the person's name whom you were going out with, as well as the time you returned back to the campus. If you were not "home" by 10:30, you could receive demerits, or marks against you, which could ultimately lead to dismissal from the college.

As you can imagine, my girlfriend and I found that very difficult. After all, we were in love, we wanted to be together as long as possible, and 10:30 seemed to come so quickly. Our dating usually consisted of going out with another couple, as not everyone had their own car. One day we came up with a brilliant revelation, which I was convinced was from God. We reasoned that although they had established a rule as to what time you had to be back on campus, they never set a limit on what time you could leave the campus. Following this brilliant revelation, we decided that we could get up at 4:30 or 5:00 in the morning, and by the time everybody else was even stirring, we were 100 miles away, enjoying breakfast at some restaurant, and looking forward to the long day ahead.

As you can imagine, when you start at about 4:30 or 5:00 in the morning, by the time 10:30 at night rolls around you are a little exhausted and ready for home. My point is, though, that love always makes a way to be with the one you want to be with.

Now the school had another rule. You had to be up early in order to have your devotional time prior to breakfast at 8:00. There were monitors assigned to the women's dormitory and the men's dormitory who would make sure you were up on time. The problem was that I was not a part of the student body as far as accommodation was concerned, because I lived in the staff quarters (even though I was never officially on the staff). This meant that I was not monitored, so I was free to sleep in. I didn't have to get up; nobody ever knew whether I had my devotions or not. I struggled to get up early to have my devotions, especially in the middle of winter when it was freezing cold and the bed was nice and warm.

You see, my relationship with God at that time was not what it should have been. My relationship with God was based on a legal obligation. I felt this was something I had to do; it was something that was placed on me. It was a control, if you like. My relationship with my girlfriend (now my wife) was a love relationship. If she suggested that we begin our dates at 2:00 in the morning, I would have had no problem bounding out of bed, all ready to go.

You see, God wants us to have a love relationship with Him. When you have a love relationship, it makes everything so much easier. If you love something, it's not a hardship. If you love golf and somebody says, "Let's go play golf," you'll drop everything to play golf. Isn't that right? If you like to go shopping, and someone says, "Let's go shopping," you don't say, "Oh, do we have to?" For our sakes and for His, God is desirous that we come into a love relationship with Him. He desires intimacy—do you?

Chapter 3

Authority

The characteristic of a saint's life is this bent of obedience, no notion of authority anywhere about it. If we begin to say, "I have been put in this position and I have to exercise authority," God will soon remove us. When there is steadfast obedience to Jesus, it is the authority of God that comes through and other souls obey at once.

—Oswald Chambers

WE now want to turn our attention to the area of authority. Dependency will drive us to intimacy, and out of intimacy comes authority. Let me say that again: Dependency, if we understand it properly, will drive us to intimacy, and from intimacy flows authority.

I remember a lady who came forward in one of my meetings a number of years ago. She was somewhat timid and quiet, and she brought with her another lady for moral support. She said,

"Brother Ravenhill, would you please pray that I will be bold and confident?"

I answered her request by saying, "No, I will not." Oh I said it in a loving and gentle way, and then I explained why. I said, "Listen, God has given you a gift, and you don't realize what that gift is. The gift is weakness, and as long as you recognize your weakness, it will drive you to God. But if I pray, and all of a sudden you have confidence and boldness in yourself, you will not need God's help anymore."

Two days later she came to me in that conference, took me by the hand, and said, "Brother Ravenhill, thank you. Nobody has ever told me that my weakness is a gift, and now that I understand it, I can honestly say it's driven me to God."

Dependency will drive us to intimacy—or it should. And out of intimacy then comes authority. Jesus said in Luke 4:18, *"The Spirit of the Lord is upon Me, because He anointed Me to preach the gospel."* We cannot do the work of the ministry without the anointing and authority that comes from total dependency and intimacy. We need the Spirit of God in order to function effectively.

Consider Jesus as the pattern Son, who Himself needed the anointing of the Spirit of God. Jesus was the Word of God incarnate, and yet was totally and completely dependent upon the Spirit anointing Him. In Acts 10:38 we have a very beautiful summary of the life of Jesus: *"You know of Jesus of Nazareth, how God anointed Him with the Holy Spirit and with power, and how He went about doing good and healing all who were oppressed by the devil, for God was with Him."*

We need God with us. The Bible talks about the early Church and how God worked with them. What a beautiful statement. That's what we need: God working with us. We need the power of God; we need the authority of God; but it comes out of relationship, it comes out of intimacy. The Bible says, *"They took notice that they had been with Jesus"* (Acts 4:13). They took notice. *You've spent time with Him, I can tell. You look like Him, you talk like Him, you walk like Him, and you act like Him.*

Become Like Your Master

Everybody is into discipleship these days. We have elevated this teaching beyond what the Scriptures teach. Most churches teach that after becoming a Christian, if you really mean business with God, you become a disciple. The fact is, in the Word of God it's totally reversed. There were all sorts of disciples in the New Testament. The Bible talks about the fact that the Pharisees said, *"We are disciples of Moses"* (John 9:28). John the Baptist had disciples, the Pharisees had disciples, Jesus had disciples, and Jesus said, *"It is enough that a disciple become as his master"* (see Matt. 10:25).

In other words, the whole purpose of discipleship is to align yourself to someone, with the intent of becoming like them. Today we would simply refer to them as a student of so and so or an understudy. For example, suppose you're gifted in music and play the violin. One of your favorite violinists offers you the opportunity of taking lessons from them, and your hope is that one day you will play as well as they do. Jesus said, *"It is enough that a disciple become as his master"* (see Matt. 10:25). In other words, a disciple is simply a student whose desire is to ultimately be like his master or tutor, somebody who sits at the feet of somebody else, wanting to become as great as they are.

The whole point of discipleship is to become like your master, and the Bible says in the Book of Acts, that the disciples were first called Christians at Antioch. What is a Christian? A Christian is a disciple who has arrived at his goal of being Christlike. You see how we've reversed it? In other words, they said, "You are

Christlike. We can tell that you've spent time with Jesus. You studied under Him, you act like Him, you walk like Him, talk like Him, clearly you're a Christian." So you don't begin as a Christian and then become a disciple. Instead, you begin as a disciple and you become a Christian, according to the Word of God.

Now I know that upsets a lot of people's theology, and I understand where they're coming from, what they're trying to emphasize. These days the word *Christian* has become very watered down, but as the Word of God reveals, it was an incredible honor to be called a Christian, a Christlike one.

Anointing and Authority

Divine authority is absolutely imperative. I've lived long enough to be exposed to all sorts of teachings that have captured the attention of the Body of Christ over the years: the discipleship movement, pageantry, prosperity, deliverance, to name but a few. Years ago there was a great emphasis placed on "church government." We were taught that the reason that we don't see New Testament churches functioning with New Testament results is that we don't have a New Testament form of church government. These teachers would emphasize the need for plurality of leaders and other government structures.

Although I believe that there was a measure of truth in what they taught, I discovered one day as I was reading in the Old Testament during my devotional time something that changed my perspective. I was reading the portion of Scripture in Exodus chapter 40, where God is speaking to Moses. By now, many months had passed since Moses had received God's pattern concerning the tabernacle, and many had worked to bring the tabernacle close to completion.

It is then that God says to Moses, "I want you to set up the tabernacle." And so the process begins. God says in Exodus 40:2-7:

On the first day of the first month you shall set up the tabernacle of the tent of meeting. You shall place the ark of the testimony there, and you shall screen the ark with the veil. You shall bring in the table and arrange what belongs on it; and you shall bring in the lampstand and mount its lamps. Moreover, you shall set the gold altar of incense before the ark of the testimony, and set up the veil for the doorway to the tabernacle. You shall set the altar of burnt offering in front of the doorway of the tabernacle.... You shall set the laver between the tent of meeting and the altar and put water in it....

Interesting the way God began, He began with the inside and worked His way out. At the end after Moses totally completes everything that God tells him to do, when everything is in it's correct place—the laver is in the right place, the brazen altar is in the right place, the altar of incense and the table of showbread are in the right place, the ark is placed in the holy of holies, and the veil is put up—everything is exactly the way God intended it. But there is one thing still missing. The same thing can be said about a New Testament pattern also. You can have a perfect New Testament church pattern with every single piece in place but yet still have something missing.

What was missing in the Old Testament tabernacle? Notice what God said after all that exacting preparation of putting everything in the appropriate place:

*Then you shall take the **anointing oil** and **anoint the tabernacle and all that is in it**, and shall consecrate it and all its furnishings; and it shall be holy. You shall anoint the altar of burnt offering and all its utensils, and consecrate the altar.... You shall anoint the laver and its stand, and consecrate it. Then you shall bring Aaron and his sons...and wash them with*

*water. You shall put the holy garments on **Aaron and anoint
him** and consecrate him, that he may minister as a priest to Me.
You shall bring **his sons...and you shall anoint them** even as
you have anointed their father, that they may minister as priests
to Me; and their anointing will qualify them for a perpetual
priesthood throughout their generations* (Exodus 40:9-15).

You see, there was one thing that was lacking. Even though
they had a structure perfectly patterned after God's purposes, it
lacked the anointing. The same goes for us today. We can have all
our theology down pat; we can have everything appear to be
right—all our ducks in a row, so to speak—and yet lack the
anointing of the Spirit of God. One of my father's favorite sayings
was, "You can have 30 degrees and still be frozen." In other words
you can earn degree after degree after degree, and Ph.D. after
Ph.D., and still be as cold as ice when you stand up to preach,
because there is no anointing, no quickening, no authority of the
Spirit of God resting upon you.

We need the authority that only God can give us. Some of you
are familiar with one of the great revivals: the revival in the
Hebrides. (The Hebrides I'm referring to are not the South Pacific
Hebrides but the Hebrides that are off the west coast of Scotland.)
Back in the late 1940s–early 1950s, this little group of islands
experienced a powerful move of the Spirit of God, one of the
purest revivals that we have seen, at least in my generation.
Seventy-five percent of the people who were saved were convert-
ed outside the walls of the church.

In other words, God came down and saturated the community with His presence. People were up all night getting right with
God. People would walk on the road and come under conviction
of sin and fall down at the side of the road, repenting of their sin.
They weren't exposed to any preaching, just the Spirit of God that
suddenly invaded the area. The revival was preceded by the

earnest praying of several young men as well as two elderly women. Their cry was that God "would rend the heavens and come down."

The people reported that five years after that revival you could count on one hand the number of people who had drifted away from God. Bars closed down; saloons closed down; dance halls closed down. The entire community was changed as a result of that revival.

One man whom God greatly used was a Presbyterian minister by the name of Duncan Campbell. Duncan Campbell was the key figure really. One night he had a dream, and in this dream he was walking into one of the small towns on the islands. As he approached the town, he noticed that there was a large crowd of people listening to somebody preaching the Word of God. As he got closer, he could hear the Word of God being proclaimed, but he didn't recognize the preacher. After a while it dawned on him that this was no ordinary preacher; this was the devil.

Finally the crowd dispersed, and in his dream he went up to the devil and said, "You're the devil, aren't you?"

"Yes I am," he replied.

Duncan Campbell then asked, "Why are you preaching the gospel? Why are you preaching the Word of God?"

And the devil responded, saying, "Duncan Campbell, don't you know that the greatest weapon I have is the preaching of the Word of God without the anointing of the Spirit? You see, the letter kills, but the Spirit gives life."

You can take a knife that doesn't have a cutting edge to it, and if you run it over your hand long enough, it will produce a callus. You will become so hardened that almost nothing will cut through. And that's what the Word of God does without the anointing of the Spirit; it produces a callousness in the lives of men and women.

I am convinced that all over America there is a lack of the anointing. People are callous to the Word of God. Oh, they know the great Bible stories; they know the basic truths of God's Word. But there is no transformation that has taken place in their life because that sharp two-edged sword has not been able to penetrate and bring conviction of sin due to the lack of the anointing. Only by the Spirit of God, as He anoints the Word of God and brings it to life, can there be any conviction. We cannot function apart from the Spirit of God.

God's Bible School

Jesus' disciples experienced the finest Bible school the world has ever known, better than any seminary: three years with the Lord Jesus Christ, not sitting there taking notes in a classroom full of students, but going on field trips every single day. They observed and learned how to cast out a demon, how to raise the dead, how to cleanse a leper, and how to feed 5,000 people. Talk about Bible school. There was no greater Bible school than that particular group of 12 students experienced. They ate with Jesus, slept near Him, walked beside Him, talked to Him, and, as John said, *"That which...we have seen with our eyes, which we have looked upon, and our hands have handled, concerning the Word of life...*[that's what we] *declare to you"* (1 John 1:1-2 NKJV).

They were constantly with Him. What an incredible school! "If you see Me," Jesus said, "you've seen the Father" (see John 14:9). Imagine spending three years in the presence of the Father, so to speak, and yet at the end of that three years, instead of getting a diploma, Jesus told you you're not ready to graduate. There is still one final requirement, "Stay in Jerusalem until you receive power from on high" (see Luke 24:49). Now if the 12 disciples needed that enduement of power from on high—how much more do you and I? We need the power of God. We need the presence of God in our lives. We are incapable of functioning without His authority.

Hebrews 1:9 speaks prophetically of the Lord Jesus Christ. It says, "You have loved righteousness and hated lawlessness; therefore God, Your God, has anointed You with the oil of gladness above Your companions." Notice the conditions: "Because you've loved righteousness and you hated lawlessness, therefore God has placed His anointing upon You." I believe that one of the keys to maintaining the anointing is that hatred of sin, that we love what God loves and hate what God hates.

Zion, the Place of God's Presence

In the Book of Isaiah we find an interesting passage of Scripture. It reads as follows: "*Look upon Zion, the city of our appointed feasts; your eyes will see Jerusalem, an undisturbed habitation, a tent which will not be folded; its stakes will never be pulled up, nor any of its cords be torn apart,*" speaking there, I believe, of David's tabernacle. That passage goes on to say, "*But there the majestic One, the Lord, will be for us a place of rivers and wide canals on which no boat with oars will go, and on which no mighty ship will pass*" (Isa. 33:20-21). Zion represents God's ideal purpose for His people. Much of God's purpose in the Old Testament revolved around Zion; it was the epitome of everything that God desired in the life of His people Israel.

Zion was the place of His presence; it was from Zion that He extended His scepter and said, "*Rule in the midst of your enemies*" (Ps. 110:2). Zion was a place of exceeding joy. As many of you know, Zion was the last stronghold to be taken by the children of Israel when they came in and systematically began to take over the land. Before then, the Jebusites controlled Zion. Why?

Because it was a natural fortress. The Bible says, *"Zion on the sides of the north"* (Ps. 48:2 KJV). In other words, it was part of Jerusalem, but it was a natural fortification. There were steep sides going up to it, so the Jebusites who controlled it could see whoever was advancing, and of course they could eliminate them because they had the advantage—they were up on top of the mountain.

You may recall how David and his men defeated the Jebusites and David claimed Zion for himself. This is *"the city of David"* (2 Sam. 5:7). It became known as Zion, the place where God desired to dwell. I believe it was a place that God intended all along. When He brought the children of Israel out of Egypt, He said, *"I'm going to take you to 'the' mountain of Mine inheritance"* (see Exod. 15:17). God had Zion in mind right from the very beginning. There was something about Zion that represented the full purposes of God.

The River of God's Presence

The Bible says that in Zion, there will be *"a place of rivers"* (Isa. 33:21). Now how many of you have ever seen a river on top of a mountain? We usually don't picture a river on top of a mountain; rivers flow down in the valley. But notice what it says, *"But there the majestic One, the Lord, will be for us a place of rivers and wide canals"* (Isa. 33:21). In other words, where the presence of God is, there is a constant river of life. You find that repeatedly all the way through the Word of God.

Every tabernacle of God has a river. There is a fascinating little book by a man named Robert Govett. Govett says that the very first tabernacle was the garden of Eden. As you are aware, out of Eden there flowed a river. In Ezekiel, from under the throne, there flowed a river. You go into the Book of Revelation, and we see there also that a river flows out from the presence of God. Govett states, "When man made the laver it was the best man could produce because, unlike God, he is incapable of producing a river. Every tabernacle that God made has a river flowing from it."

So here in Zion we have a river. The river is, of course, God's presence. *"There the majestic One, the Lord, will be for us a place of rivers."* And then it says this, *"On which no boat with oars will go, and on which no mighty ship will pass"* (Isa. 33:21).

In other words, there is one restriction. If we are to enter into the river of God, the presence of God, one thing is banned: rowboats, mighty ships. These were the great ships with their galley slaves, like you see in Ben Hur. These rowboats, mighty ships, were propelled by human energy, human strength, human power, human skill and expertise. And God says, "If you are to understand My presence, there is no human effort required."

You see, a lot of us, myself included, have a piece of paper, a diploma, that says that we graduated from "rowing school." I was taught how to counsel, how to preach, and how to expound the Word of God. We teach people the "how-tos," and God says, "not in Zion."

Isaiah goes on to state, *"Your tackle hangs slack; it cannot hold the base of its mast firmly, nor spread out the sail"* (Isa. 33:23). In other words, the complaint seems to be, "You guys are good rowers, but you're not good sailors." There is all the difference in the world between a rowboat and a sailboat; one is extremely hard work. How many of you have ever rowed a boat? Especially if you've got an old clunker of a boat and there's a little bit of a breeze, it's incredible the amount of energy that it takes to move a rowboat.

How many of you have ever been in a sailboat? You put up the sail and, other than the occasional sail adjustment, the wind does everything for you. I believe that one of the things the church needs, and I need it as much as anybody else, is to learn how to put up a sail—because I don't know about you, but I'm tired of rowing. Like the disciples who told Jesus, *"We've toiled all night and caught nothing, nevertheless at Your word"* (Luke 5:4-5), and they let down the nets.

Can you imagine a professional fisherman taking advice from a carpenter on how to fish? "Lord, we know. We've been doing this all our lives. We know, we know, there's nothing out there right now. They're not biting. I mean, we've toiled all night, you know. We haven't just been out there for an hour or so; we've been out there all night."

He says, "Let's do it My way." And we need to do it His way. You see, my way of doing it is exhausting. My way of counseling takes forever. But when God gives you a word of knowledge, all of a sudden everything changes.

Experiencing the Prophetic Realm

I've been deeply challenged in the last couple of years by a wonderful brother from England who moves in the prophetic realm. He has told some of the most amazing stories I think I've ever come across, as to the way the Spirit of God operates and the spiritual potential that is available to those who truly wait upon Him.

He tells the story of being invited to a church in England. Following the Sunday morning service, the pastor invites him to his house for dinner. When he arrives at the house he is introduced to some of the church elders, as well to a young lady whom he is told is soon going to be sent out by the church as a missionary to China. Following the meal, the pastor then asks if he would pray for the lady. First, however, the young woman shared her vision for China and what she hoped to be doing. It was then time to pray. Immediately the man bowed his head, and the Lord spoke a clear word into his spirit. "Tell her I hate mommies and daddies." This man has a good sense of humor and thought to himself, *Sometimes I detest this gift. Why can't I be a teacher?* The Lord, however, kept impressing this thought upon his mind, "Tell her I hate mommies and daddies."

He then shared some valuable insight into the "prophetic" realm. He said, "The mind receives information, the spirit receives revelation, and the mind and the spirit don't always agree." The Bible says, "The natural mind understands not the things of the Spirit of God, because they are foolishness" (see 1 Cor. 2:14). And his mind was saying, "This is foolishness. This doesn't make sense. Why should I tell her that You hate mommies and daddies? God, You made mommies and daddies. I don't understand what it means, but obviously You made mommies and daddies, and I'm not going to embarrass myself by saying that You hate mommies and daddies. I can't." His mind could not fathom what the Lord was saying to him.

Not wanting to give the word because he doesn't understand it, he stalls for time hoping the Lord will release him and give him another word. This causes the pastor to think that he hasn't made himself clear, so he says, "If God gives you a word, feel free to share it."

The man looks at the young lady, and says, "God has told me one thing. He wants you to know that He hates mommies and daddies." Suddenly, all the color drains out of her face, and she became livid and lunged at him. He prayed, and she collapsed in a heap on the floor. A little while later they begin to talk to her, and for the first time in her life she begins to open up some very deep wounds, and she said, "When I was a little girl for many, many years, my grandfather, two uncles, and a friend used to sexually abuse me. When my grandfather used to come into the room, he would always take the lead, and he would say to me, 'We are going to play mommies and daddies.'"

God said, "Tell her I hate mommies and daddies."

All of a sudden, all that pain, she was able to get free of. She had carried it, the shame, the embarrassment of not being able to express to anybody what she'd been through, and yet there was a call of God upon her life. Here she was, wanting to serve God, and yet in a sense she was bearing this heavy burden. Suddenly she was set free.

You see, you can counsel all day, and "row" all night, and not make any headway. But just one word from God and all of a sudden that girl was set free. We need the Spirit of God, don't we?

This man tells another story about going into a supermarket one day to buy some cheese. He goes up to the deli counter, and as he's approaching, he sees a lady behind it, and God says to him, "This lady does not know Me, but last night she prayed to a God she doesn't know even exists, because she is desperate. She's got a daughter she hasn't seen in four years. They've had a falling out. Her daughter has left home, and all she knows is that her daughter is in London somewhere. She doesn't know if she's dead or alive, selling drugs, or into prostitution, and last night she got down and said, 'God, if there is a God, bring my daughter back.'"

The man goes up to the lady, and of course the lady is there to serve, and she says, "Sir, can I help you?"

And he says, "Well, before you do, I'd like you to know that I'm a Christian. This may not mean anything to you, but God told me that last night you prayed to a God you're not even sure exists, because you've got a daughter you haven't seen for four years."

She starts to cry. As he is talking to her, God gives him another word, so he says, "Listen, this week, on Wednesday at 2 o'clock in the afternoon, your daughter will call you." (I'm not sure those are the exact words he used, but I do know that he gave her a specific day and time that her daughter would call her.)

That lady was so touched because of the power of that prophetic word, and that word of knowledge. *After all*, she thought, *how could anybody know what I did last night in the privacy of my own home?* She went home, after rearranging her schedule, and made herself a cup of tea, sat down on her couch and waited. At exactly the time the man had said, the phone rang, and it was her daughter from London.

According to him, both the lady and her daughter are part of the Kingdom of God today. Both were transformed by the power of God. After the mother told the daughter what had happened, the daughter received the Lord.

Then the daughter tells her side of the story. She was walking down the street in London, totally oblivious to anything but herself, and she passes by a telephone booth. In her mind spontaneously arises this overwhelming urge to call her mother, so she walks in, picks up the phone, and calls. Obviously the Spirit of God came on that girl at the right time and placed within her the desire to contact her mother.

You see, you can row all day and accomplish little. God wants to release His presence. *"In the last days I'll pour out My Spirit, old men will dream dreams, young men will see visions..."* (see Acts 2:17). We desperately need the presence of God, and we need to allow the wind of the Spirit to fill the sails. We need to learn how to listen. I need to learn how to listen, how to cooperate with the Spirit of God.

Learn to Listen to God's Spirit

The Spirit of God often speaks in little seed form. When Jesus sowed the seed (parable of the sower), some seed produced 30-, 60-, and 100-fold. Many times God speaks just a little whisper, gives just a little seed, just something that He drops in our spirit, and we've got to learn to cultivate that. Yet the natural mind so often rationalizes everything, doesn't it?

When God enables us to move in or experience the prophetic, it can be so powerful. I can tell you story after story. Here's an example from my own life.

My wife and I were married in 1964. Following our honeymoon we drove to New York City to commence our ministry together working with David Wilkerson. We'd only been there a short time when my father asked us to come to a small gathering he was having in his living room. He had met a very unusual man who was highly gifted in the prophetic realm. I believe he was traveling in those days with the Full Gospel Businessmen.

When we arrived at his apartment, there were a number of other Teen Challenge workers there, maybe 15 or 20 of us, and this man shared the Word and then began to minister to various ones. I was over in the corner of the room, kneeling, my head was buried in my hands, and I was not uttering a single word, but deep inside me I was crying out, "God, give me wisdom."

I have two brothers, my younger has since passed away but at that stage he was still alive. They were both extremely bright, straight-A students. My younger brother earned a Ph.D. while I was the one who brought home F's on my report card on more than one occasion.

Anyway, I was crying out, "God, I need wisdom. I've been filled with the Spirit, but Lord, I need wisdom." Now I was not saying a thing audibly. I was not even moving my lips. It was just a deep cry. Within about five seconds of my crying like that, internally, I felt some hands on my head. It was this man, and the first thing he said was, "God has seen your desire for wisdom; He's giving it to you."

I immediately broke into a thousand pieces and began to weep. He then proceeded to say, "I see you, speaking into a microphone. God is going to take you before kings and rulers." I thought, *Oh great, this guy is really off the mark.* As one pastor friend would say, "He's adding a little bit of Hamburger Helper." You know what that is? You get your ground hamburger and perhaps there is not enough to go around so you mix in some more ingredients in order to make it stretch. "A lot of people, when they prophesy, add a little bit of Hamburger Helper." You can tell when the prophecy comes to an end, but then they keep on going.

So I thought, *Now he's adding a little bit of Hamburger Helper.*

It seemed impossible to me that God would take me before kings and rulers. The man continued, "I can see a vision of you right now. In front of you there's a huge field, and there are literally hundreds and hundreds and hundreds of people with brown skin sitting before you on the grass. These people have brown skin," he went on to say.

Two years later my wife and I left New York for New Zealand. We were involved with Youth With A Mission (YWAM), in the beginning days of their ministry there. I joined the very first team on an outreach to the Pacific Islands. But it was on the second team that we linked up with some teams from America and traveled to the island of Tonga. Tonga is possibly one of the smallest island groups in the Pacific Ocean and certainly one of the smallest kingdoms in the world.

We arrived just a couple of weeks prior to the time of the coronation of the king. The Queen had died, and now it was time for the coronation. The Methodist church had asked different members of the team to speak at a special gathering they had every week. The Methodist church is the national church of Tonga, and they had a policy of inviting any visiting dignitaries to speak at their large weekly outdoor meetings.

During the first two weeks, two of the team members were asked to speak. I was asked to speak the third week. The third week was the week of the coronation of the king, and they decided to change the venue to a field adjacent to the king's palace. Now we're not talking about a palace like Buckingham Palace or anything like that, or one of Saddam Hussein's palaces, we're talking about something similar to a Southern mansion with a picket fence around it. The "palace" was situated just a short distance away from the main town.

I stood up to speak and the palace was directly behind me. In front of me there were literally hundreds and hundreds of Tongans, brown-skinned, sitting cross-legged on the grass, just the same way that man had described it two years prior, there in the middle of New York City. After I had finished speaking, some of the kids came up to me and the YWAMers and said, "Guess what? Guess what?"

They were all excited. I said, "What?"

They said, "The king stood behind you on his veranda and listened to you speak."

All of a sudden that prophetic word came back to me, and the clarity of it was amazing. I realized that I was in the very center of the will of God right now, right in this place, because two years ago God gave me that word.

See, God is able to do amazing things, isn't He? I could give you examples of other incidents like that. I've always been deeply, deeply impacted by people who move under the true anointing of the Spirit of God, who have ears to hear and are willing to step out in faith, and it makes all the difference in the world.

Some years ago I left a church of about 550 people. We had 16 acres of land, a beautiful building, and a school—all of that, and I left. I handed the whole thing over to another man, no strings attached, and I stepped out into an itinerant ministry. What made the stepping easier was that I'd had a few prophetic words and a deep sense of what God wanted me to do.

I was attending a large conference in Kansas where a man who moved in the prophetic realm was ministering. I had fasted and prayed asking the Lord for one final confirmation that I was doing the right thing. Out of a crowd of some 4,000, this man called my wife and I out: "Would David and Nancy Ravenhill please stand." And we stood up.

He gave a brief word about my father and explained to the crowd that he knew us both but that he had not seen us for about five years. He then said, "David, I have a word of direction for you. God is going to bless your traveling and itinerant ministry." All it took was that one little phrase, and I knew, exactly, that what God wanted me to do was travel and give up the church. I'm doing that today—again based partly on a prophetic word. It was a word of confirmation.

Earnestly Desire Spiritual Gifts

My father used to say, "Psychiatry and psychology are man's substitute for the gifts of the Spirit." You can go to the "shrink" and lie down on his couch while he tries to unravel your problem. "Tell me about this" and "Tell me about that," he'll say, hoping somehow to find the key to your problem.

A true word of knowledge can immediately go to the root of the problem. "When you were five years of age, you were molested by your uncle." *Boom*. There is no substitute for the gifts of the Spirit; they are the "tools of the trade." We need to earnestly desire spiritual gifts, and I mean earnestly desire spiritual gifts. There are seasons in my life when I get before God and I say, "God, I do not want to stand before You one day and hear You say, 'I had many things to tell you, many things to give you, which you never sought Me about.'"

I know my basic gifting is teaching, but I don't want to stand there and hear the Lord say, "David, I could have given you all of this as well, but you never sought Me." I would rather seek Him and not get it, than not seek Him and find out that He had it for me.

We need to earnestly pursue spiritual gifts, not so that we'll be famous men or women of God who operate in the word of knowledge, prophecy, or whatever—no, for the sake of the Body. The gifts are always for somebody else. If I have a healing gift, it's because my brother is sick. If I have a word of knowledge, it's because my sister needs a word of knowledge. If I have a word of wisdom, it's because somebody else needs a word of wisdom. It's for the sake of the Body, and the Body is suffering because we do not have the God-given tools.

In First Corinthians chapter 12, we have this wonderful chapter on the gifts of the Spirit, but I want you to notice the way Paul introduces this chapter: *"Now concerning spiritual gifts, brethren, I do not want you to be unaware* [or ignorant]" (1 Cor. 12:1). Now Paul is not just talking about having all the facts; he's basically saying, "Listen, you need this. I don't want you to be ignorant of these things."

Paul continues, *"You know that when you were pagans,"* in other words, when you were unsaved, your former life, *"you were led astray to the mute* [dumb] *idols, however you were led. Therefore, I make known to you that no one speaking by the Spirit of God says, 'Jesus is accursed,'"* (1 Cor. 12:2-3) and so on.

Notice the contrast. Prior to their accepting Christ, he says to the Corinthians, "You used to go into temples, you were caught up in idolatry, and your paganism," and he says, "there was one defining thing about those pagan gods—they were *dumb*." Now today we use the word *dumb* to mean stupid, not very bright or intelligent. But Paul is not referring to it in that way. He's saying to the Corinthians, "The majority of your life, as heathens, you worshiped a god that could not *communicate*. You would go to them with your bowl of rice, or some such offering, hoping to *hear* from your god, and yet you went away never hearing a word because you were worshiping a dumb idol."

In the Old Testament we have many descriptions of idols. One of them is in the Book of Psalms where it describes an idol as a scarecrow in a cucumber patch, to keep the birds away. It's dressed to look like a man. *"It has eyes, but it can't see, ears but it can't hear, a mouth but it can't **speak**"* (Jer. 10:5).

Paul is drawing a contrast here with their past gods and the living and true God they now serve. He states, *"I make known to you that no one **speaking** by the Spirit of God says…"* (1 Cor. 12:3). In other words, the God that you worship now is a God who *communicates*, He *speaks*, as opposed to your old gods who never spoke to you. Paul then reveals to the church that God communicates His power through healing. The way He communicates His encouragement is through a prophetic word; the way He communicates His wisdom is through a word of wisdom; the way He communicates His knowledge is through a word of knowledge.

He's a God who wants to speak. He wants to declare His love, compassion, and goodness. One of the great tragedies in the Church of Jesus Christ today is that we have a *dumb* god. It's time for the Church to rediscover the fact that God longs to speak to

His Church. He speaks primarily through His Word, but not only His Word. He also speaks through the various gifts of the Holy Spirit.

John 7:37-38 says, *"On the last day, the great day of the feast, Jesus stood and cried out, saying, 'If anyone is thirsty, let him come to Me and drink. He who believes in Me, as the Scripture said, from his innermost being will flow rivers of living water.'"* I know we are all familiar with that verse, as I've been familiar with it for many, many years.

When I travel, I carry with me a personal digital assistant (PDA), and on that PDA I have the entire Bible, including Strong's Concordance. One day I was reading this particular portion of Scripture and I highlighted "innermost being." If you have the King James Version, it's translated as "belly." On my PDA when I highlight a word or phrase it gives you the Greek word, and it tells you the various renderings of the word. The way this Greek word is translated by far the most is as the word "womb." Think about that, what a fascinating verse.

That verse is basically saying, "If any man is barren, if any man is thirsty, let him come to Me, and I will open his womb, and out of it will flow rivers of...," of what? "Life."

You see, you and I are spiritually barren until the Spirit of God opens our womb. We cannot conceive; we cannot give birth; we cannot bring forth what God wants us to bring forth in our own strength, in our own energy. We can row all day, but accomplish little. However, when the Spirit of God opens your womb, you can conceive and give birth. I had never in 40 years of ministry ever seen that before, but you can check it out. It's the word "womb."

Barrenness was always considered a curse in the Bible. It was a stigma that many women had to endure. Rachel said, *"Give me children, or else I die"* (Gen. 30:1). She couldn't bear the rejection of not having the ability to conceive. All eyes were upon her as she made her way around town. People would no doubt scorn her and ridicule her because in their minds God had put a curse on her by not giving her any children. And she says, "I'm going to die unless You open my womb." We too are going to die unless God opens the womb of the Church.

"If anyone is thirsty, let him come to Me and drink" (John 7:37). There dwells in Zion the Majestic One who will be to us a place of rivers—a life-giving river. I don't know about you, but I know that I'm getting thirstier and thirstier these days, especially as I come across men and women who have moved in the supernatural realm. Now I'm aware that God gives gifts as He wills, and I know that we're not all the same member of the Body; there are different members. But we need to see a new generation of believers raised up who are not going to give God any rest until they see a fresh move of the Spirit.

Paul exhorted the believers in Corinth to *"desire earnestly spiritual gifts"* (1 Cor. 14:1). It may take fasting and crying out to God before we see an answer, but think of the blessing not only to the Church but to the world!

I pray almost on a daily basis for God to restore the Church to true apostolic power and purity. Something has to change. We're seeing the enemy coming in like a flood, and the Church is largely powerless to do anything about it. We need men and women who walk in the full authority of the Spirit of God. This was the promise that Jesus left to the Church: *"You will receive power when the Holy Spirit has come upon you"* (Acts 1:8). This divine authority comes from knowing God; it comes from spending time in His presence. Dependency leads to intimacy and intimacy leads to authority.

Chapter 4

Persistency

Persist: to stand or be fixed; to go on resolutely in spite of opposition, importunity or warning, tenacious, enduring, perseverance.

—Noah Webster, American Dictionary

You may suffer, you may bleed, you may break, but you shall go on.

—Catherine Booth-Clibborn

If one door seems hopelessly closed against you, undaunted you will hammer at another; if your way is blocked to Asia, you will be sure that there is a post for you in America. A post for you somewhere you are convinced there is, and you will never rest until you find it. If you cannot get at the crowds from the platform, you will plead with them in the street; if you are unable to speak with them in multitudes, you will the more zealously deal with the individual; in short, whether in train or car, at the back door or in your sick room, you will feel the instinct of the shepherd, your heart will go out in compassion, and you will be impelled to serve.

—Emma Booth-Tucker

To save the world is our desire,
For enemies we pray;
We'll never tire, we'll stand the fire,
And never, never run away.

—William Pearson

"JESUS...*who for the joy set before Him endured the cross*" (Heb. 12:2). If Jesus was tempted in all points like we are, then I'm sure there were times when He felt as if He couldn't go on any longer. He probably heard rumors from early childhood that He was "illegitimate." He spent 40 days alone in the wilderness being tempted by none other than the devil himself. He was rejected by the very ones He came to save. People compared Him to Beelzebub. He was despised by the religious people of His day and finally subjected to the most horrific scourging and crucifixion that we can possibly conceive of. And yet He remained "*steadfast, immovable, always abounding in the work of the Lord*" (1 Cor. 15:58). This leads us to another key principle to surviving the anointing: PERSISTENCY.

Don't Look Back

By persistency I mean that tenacity of spirit whereby we refuse to give up regardless of our circumstances, regardless of the pressure that we may be surrounded with. Like Paul said, *"Forgetting those things which are behind, I press on"* (see Phil. 3:13-14). Jesus set His *"face like flint"* (Isa. 50:7). Nothing was going to deter Him; nothing was going to distract Him. He was determined to finish the course that God had set before Him. I believe that is what God is looking for in our lives, that determination not to get sidetracked, but to keep going, "putting your hand to the plow and not looking back" (see Luke 9:62).

So many people begin well, but they do not end well, and that is one of the great tragedies today in the Christian world. In the second book I wrote, titled *They Drank From the River and Died in the Wilderness*, I recount the story of Israel's great deliverance from Egypt. Approximately a million people came out of Egypt. Every single one of them began well; every single one of them began the race. However, the "finishing line," if you like, was in the land of Canaan, yet only two out of that million people made it—not a very good retention rate. Two out of a million people made it across the finishing line. Moses himself did not make it and died in the wilderness.

Paul recalls Israel's great exodus in First Corinthians chapter 9 and 10. In Chapter 9 he introduces the illustration of a race, *"We all run the race,"* and then he says, *"run in such a way that you may win"* (1 Cor. 9:24). He goes on then to personalize it, saying, *"I run in such a way that I might win. I buffet my body; I bring it in subjection. I deal with it when my body wants to do something; my spirit says you can't do it"* (see 1 Cor. 9:24-27). He ruled over the desires of the flesh. And then he goes right into chapter 10. In the original text, of course, there are no chapter divisions, so he continues with his illustration by saying, *"I don't want you to be ignorant, all our fathers started in the race."*

Paul says, "They all started." The race began in Egypt; the finishing line was the land of Canaan, but they never made it. They died in the wilderness. Why did they die? Because of immorality, because of murmuring and disobedience and unbelief at God's word and so on. Paul gives all the reasons, and he says, *"These things are written for us, upon whom the end of the age have come"* (see 1 Cor. 10:11). In other words, "This is very pertinent, very relevant to our generation here at the end of the age," and Paul goes right back to the beginning and applies it to us.

We are living in a time in which the enemy is out to sabotage what God is doing in the lives of His people. Satan is trying to bring discouragement, doubt, fears, insecurities, and everything else into our life to get us to drop out of the race, rather than go on with God.

Recognize the Seasons of Life

One of the things that will help us to "finish the race" is the realization that the Christian life is made up of seasons. In Genesis, after the flood, God came to Noah and gave him a promise. The promise was that as long as the earth remains, there will be *"seedtime and harvest, and cold and heat, and summer and winter, and day and night shall not cease"* (Gen. 8:22). Notice the contrast between seedtime and harvest. Seedtime is a time when the land is dry and barren; it's got to be plowed up. There is no life. The rough, hard soil has to be tilled and cultivated. Then you've got harvest time, where there is all the lush fruit and the wheat, or whatever it is that you've planted. What a contrast between the two!

You have "cold and heat," again a contrast between two things. *"Summer and winter, and day and night shall not cease"* (Gen.

8:22). And of course the Bible says, *"First...the natural; then the spiritual"* (1 Cor. 15:46). We need to understand that in the Christian life there are these different seasons. Once we understand that, it helps enable us somewhat to be able to go through those seasons without becoming discouraged or defeated.

I will never forget the first graduation that we had in the Brownsville Revival School of Ministry there in Pensacola, Florida. The school began as a result of the revival. I believe the first intake of students was around 70-80 students, and within three years it had grown to 1,200 students. I was privileged to have taught at the school for a short period of time. At that first graduation ceremony, I sat on the podium alongside the other "professors." Pastor John Kilpatrick, the senior pastor of the church there in Brownsville, addressed the graduating students.

To illustrate the point he was making, Kilpatrick said, "I want you to picture an old-fashioned harbor, and around the harbor there is a wall with a narrow opening to allow the ship to pass through. There, tied up at the jetty or the wharf, is a boat, an old sailing boat. The boat is being loaded with all types of provisions and goods. People are loading the vessel with crates and sacks of supplies. The boat is almost fully loaded, creating tremendous excitement. The reason is, there are a number of new crew members who are going out for their very first voyage. They've never been to sea before, hence their excitement." Pastor Kilpatrick continued, "As you look out across the harbor, everything is calm and placid, not a ripple on the water. It is the type of scene you see on postcards."

After describing the harbor he continued, "That's the way I see you students. For the last two years you've been taking on cargo. You've been sitting under the ministry of men and women of God; you've been receiving the richness of God's Word. Day after day you have been loading your vessel with the cargo, the truth of

God's Word. Tomorrow you are going to set sail, and there's great excitement. Some of you have never been out in the ministry before. Some of you are going to the mission field; some of you are going to pastor churches; some of you are going out as worship leaders; others are going out as youth pastors, and you cannot wait. It's almost time for your ship to set sail."

By now the students are listening intently. He continued, "The morning comes and the boat is ready to set sail. Slowly it moves out of the harbor. There's just a slight breeze as the ship pulls away from the wharf and heads toward the entrance of the harbor. Once out in the open sea the boat heads toward its ultimate destination." He paused for a moment, then went on, "I can guarantee you that these calm, placid conditions won't remain for long. Pretty soon the winds are going to increase, and before long you're going to be in the midst of a storm. All hell is going to break loose around you, and you're going to wonder, you're going to doubt, 'Did I really have a call to be a sailor? Is this really what I thought "ministry" is all about?'"

As I listened to him share that illustration, I thought, *Here is a seasoned man of God*. What does that mean? When we talk about a well-seasoned man of God, or a well-seasoned woman of God, we are referring to a man or a woman of God who has gone through hardship and trials, rejection, accusations, and suffering, and yet they've been able to face those things by the grace of God and come through victoriously, unwavering in their faith. That's what God is looking for in our life.

Don't Despise a Season of Suffering

We sometimes read about missionaries from back in the days when it would take weeks or months to arrive at their "field." Then, having arrived, they would be cut off from the outside world—apart from the occasional letter that would take forever to arrive. These saints of whom the world is not worthy would suffer hardship beyond description. Many would bury their precious children who died due to the lack of medical facilities. Others would stand by the grave of a spouse, having then to face the future alone and without their mate. Yet, despite these incredibly difficult challenges, they remained steadfast in their determination to serve their God wholeheartedly. These things they understood to be part of the price they had to be willing to pay. I'm sure there were many, many times when they would take comfort in Paul's admonition to Timothy when he wrote, *"Suffer hardship with me, as a good soldier of Christ Jesus"* (2 Tim. 2:3).

Today we live in a society where the slightest little difficulty causes us to turn and run. We become so easily upset and discouraged, allowing self-pity to rob us of the opportunity of proving God in the situation.

In the Book of Revelation we are introduced to the Bride of Christ, and it says that the Bride is also the city—the city that comes down out of Heaven, having 12 gates for those wanting to enter "her." What is interesting about those gates is the substance they are made of. They're not made of gold or bronze or iron or steel. They're not made of diamonds or rubies; they're made of only one thing: *pearl*. Those gates are made of pearl. What is a pearl? A pearl is a problem that has been "overcome." I believe God knew exactly what He was doing when He revealed this to John. God didn't randomly choose pearl as opposed to iron. He was forever trying to reveal to us that the "Bride" He is looking for is able, by His grace, to transform the nitty-gritty problems of life into something of beauty and value.

You see, God is looking for a company of overcomers. Jesus Christ had to overcome—overcome all the rejection, overcome all the pain, sorrow, and sufferings along with the diabolical schemes of the devil himself. And yet nothing deterred Him. He set His face like a flint to go to Jerusalem, to finish the course that God had set before Him. God is looking for overcomers who will follow the example of His Son.

If you take a pearl and split it in half, in the middle you will find a little bit of grit or sand. Before the pearl was formed, that little irritant got into the oyster's shell, and the oyster overcomes it by covering it with a substance we know as pearl. Once overcome, that irritant becomes a thing highly valued and sought after. Some of the greatest men and women of God are the men and women of God who have suffered. Yet that suffering, when rightly responded to, produces a depth of character that reflects the very nature and beauty of Christ.

We are told in the Book of James, "*When all kinds of trials and temptations crowd into your lives, my brothers, don't resent them as intruders, but welcome them as friends. Realize that they have come to test your faith and to produce in you that quality of endurance* [persistency]. *But let the process go on until that endurance is fully developed, and you will find you have become men of mature character...*" (see James 1:2-4). Maturity comes by applying the Word of God through His grace to the situation you're facing.

If I remember correctly, it was Bob Mumford, who many years ago talked about his own spiritual development as a young believer. He likened his experience to the 23rd Psalm, "*The Lord is my shepherd; I shall not want*" (Ps. 23:1). He shared about how, when he was first saved, he went through an "I shall not want" period. He said, "All he had to do if he needed something was basically click his fingers and God was there." I think he was in college at the time, Bible college, and he had forgotten to buy an alarm clock, and so he simply said, "Lord, I need an alarm clock," and within a matter of half an hour somebody was knocking on his door asking, "Bob, do you need an alarm clock? I've got two of them."

To Bob, the Christian life was so amazing; God was so real. But then he said he had to learn that there was a progression to the Christian's walk with God. *"He makes me lie down in green pastures...beside quiet waters"* (Ps. 23:2). What an idyllic situation. Wouldn't we all love to stay there? However, the Christian life is not free from hardship. Bob went on to explain how he had to go through *"the valley of the shadow of death"* (Ps. 23:4) in order to realize that the Lord had not forsaken him but was still there walking beside him. Finally he shared how even *"in the midst of his enemies"* God had prepared for him *"a table"* (see Ps. 23:5). Yes, there are seasons in the Christian life. Each season is ordained of God and shows us His sufficiency in each and every "season of the soul."

It's not always just settling down beside still cool waters, but facing adversity, trials, and hardship. We see this in the life of Paul. As you read about his life you realize the incredible suffering that he went through. *"In far more labors, in far more imprisonments, beaten times without number, often in danger of death. Five times I received from the Jews thirty-nine lashes. Three times I was beaten with rods, once I was stoned, three times I was shipwrecked, a night and a day I have spent in the deep. I have been on frequent journeys, in dangers from rivers, danger from robbers, dangers from my countrymen, dangers from the Gentiles, dangers in the city, dangers in the wilderness, dangers on the sea, dangers among false brethren; I have been in labor and hardship, through many sleepless nights, in hunger and thirst, often without food, in cold and exposure"* (2 Cor. 11:23-27). To which he adds, *"There is the daily pressure on me of concern for all the churches"* (2 Cor. 11:28). Wow! Next time you're about to complain, consider your "problem" alongside Paul's and repent.

Paul was a *"man [of] like passions as we are"* (James 5:17). When he was whipped, he felt the pain. He knew what it was to suffer unjustly, and yet he says, in effect, "It does not deter me from what God wants to accomplish in and through my life." We likewise should be those sort of individuals who refuse to be deterred, regardless of circumstances. There will be trials and troubles, and especially as we head into these last days. I believe there's going to be an increase of persecution against the Church that we need to be prepared for—I really do.

Jesus promised us, *"You will be hated by all nations because of My name"* (Matt 24:9). The Church is going to experience a world-wide hatred, evidenced by persecution, in these last days. I am convinced of that. As it says in Psalm 2:2-3, *"The kings of the earth...take counsel together against the Lord and against His Anointed, saying: 'Let us tear their fetters apart and cast away their cords from us!'"* I understand that to mean that the Church is the only last restraining voice on the earth crying out against injustice, lawlessness, and sin. We are to be salt seeking to retard corruption, the light seeking to dispel darkness, and yet the world "loves darkness rather than light" (see John 3:19) and therefore does all within its power to cast off the *fetters* and *cords* that seek to restrain them—things like abortion and homosexuality, to name just a couple.

As you can see, the need for perseverance or persistency is essential in these days in which we are living. God will permit and allow trials, difficulties, and problems for His ultimate purposes and our good. Moses reminded the children of Israel, after their trials in the wilderness, that God said it was *"To do good for you in the end"* (Deut. 8:16).

Recently I was reading again the story of Peter, which I like to embellish a little bit in the retelling—without distorting the facts, of course. The story begins with the devil coming to pay a visit to Jesus. The scenario went something like this.

There's a knock on the door early one morning, maybe 5:00 in the morning, and Jesus answers the door. A while later Peter gets up and comes down, rubbing his eyes, still half asleep, and he says, "Lord, how long have You been up?"

"Oh, I've been up several hours."

Peter says, "Early this morning I heard a knock on the door. I thought I did anyway."

Jesus responds, "Yeah, you're right. There was a knock."

"I thought so," Peter replies. "Who on earth was coming at that hour of the morning?"

Jesus answers, "It was the devil."

"The devil?" (I can see Peter's mind racing in a thousand directions—amazed at what he's hearing.) "The devil! Really, Lord, You're not joking, are You?"

"No, it was the devil."

"The devil, what did he want?"

"Well, actually Peter, he came about you."

"Now, Lord, You are joking, aren't You? You know, Lord, I had a rough night last night."

Jesus says, "No, I'm not joking. He came about you."

"Well, what did he want?"

"Well, Peter, actually he wants to sift you like wheat. You know those great millstones that they use to grind the wheat? Well, he wants to put you between those huge stones and grind you for a while."

"Oh Lord, am I ever glad You answered the door. I guess You told him where to go, didn't You?"

"No," Jesus says.

"What do You mean 'No'? What did You tell him?"

"I said, 'Go ahead.'"

"You what?"

"I told him to go ahead," Jesus says. "I gave him permission."

I can imagine Peter looking at the Lord in total disbelief and shock. (What a friend we have in Jesus?)

Then Jesus says to Peter, "I'm praying for you, because it's going to do something that can't be accomplished any other way. It's going to put some character in you—you're going to be strengthened as a result of this. I'm going to pray that you come through able to minister to others more effectively."

Even Paul said, *"There was a time when we 'despaired even of life' itself"* (2 Cor. 1:8). But then drawing from his own experience he writes, *"God of all comfort, who comforts us in all our affliction...able to comfort those in any affliction..."* (2 Cor. 1:3-4).

God's Word reveals clearly that we are in the midst of a spiritual warfare. The enemy is unrelenting in his attack against us. Our only hope of winning is to take up *"the full armor of God that we may be able to stand against all the wiles/schemes/plans/strategies of the devil"* (see Eph. 6:11). We need to constantly remain clothed with the armor of God, having put on the helmet of salvation and the breastplate of righteousness, with our loins gird about with truth, taking up the sword of the Spirit and the shield of faith, and having our feet shod with the gospel of peace (see Eph. 6:11-17).

Count the Cost

One of my favorite Bible characters is Abraham. As you know, Abraham is the father of all those who believe. He is the prototype, if you like, the example, the model of what God is looking for in the life of every man and woman of God. We find that in chapter 15 of Genesis, Abraham is without an heir, he doesn't have any children, and he is complaining or explaining that to the Lord. Abraham says in Genesis 15:3, *"Since You have given no off-spring to me, one born in my house is my heir."* In other words, "When I die, I have no one to leave my estate to but my servant Eliezer."

> *Then behold, the word of the Lord came to him, saying, "This man will not be your heir; but one who will come forth from your own body, he shall be your heir." And He took him outside and said, "Now look toward the heavens, and count the stars, if you are able to count them." And He said to him, "So shall your descendants be." Then he believed in the Lord; and He reckoned it to him as righteousness* (Genesis 15:4-6).

Genesis 15:7 says, *"I am the Lord who brought you out of Ur of the Chaldeans, to give you this land to possess it."* So God gave Abraham two promises in this particular chapter—one being that all the land he had passed through would be his. Abraham was a type of New Testament disciple. Abraham was the prototype of what God is looking for in your life and my life. He was the first disciple. Discipleship is not just a New Testament teaching, but we find it embodied in the Old Testament. What was the first thing God had to do with Abraham? Get him to forsake his father, mother, brother, sister, and home.

Recall how the Lord promised His disciples, *"Everyone who has left houses or brothers or sisters or father or mother or children or farms for My name's sake, will receive many times as much, and will inherit eternal life"* (Matt. 19:29). God basically says to Abraham, "You who have forsaken his land and country—I will give you this land as far as your eyes can see." But He also says, "You're going to have a child."

Now Abraham is like most of us. He begins to question, "How is it possible that these things are going to happen?" After all, he's 100 years of age.

He says, "Lord, how shall I know that I shall possess it?" First of all we have the *promise*. The promise basically is that "You're going to have land"; the promise is that "You're going to have a son and your descendants are going to be like the stars of Heaven. Look up into the heavens; count the stars. If you can count them, then you have some sort of understanding of how many descendants you're going to have."

But after the promise there is always a *price* tag. So after the promise comes the price God says, *"I want you to 'bring Me a three year old heifer, a three year old goat, and a three year old ram, and a turtledove, and a young pigeon"* (Gen. 15:9). In other words, there is always a cost involved. There is always sacrifice involved in obtaining the promises of God. Although we can read this in a matter of minutes, or even seconds, we have to realize that there is a process here. Abraham has to go out, he has to inspect the various animals, and he has to bring the very best because God would not accept anything that was blemished in any way. He has to prepare them, then he has to build two altars, because they're going to ratify a covenant.

After Abraham does all that, he brings all these things to Him, and he cut the animals in two, *"laid each half opposite the other; but he did not cut the birds"* (Gen. 15:10). So Abraham has now fulfilled explicitly the Word of God. He's done exactly what God required of him, but instead of having God show up to ratify the covenant, or to ratify the promise, something else happens. Genesis 15:11 says the *predators* came: *"The birds of prey came down upon the carcasses, and Abram drove them away"* in order to preserve what he has placed on the altar. So, instead of God showing up, the enemy shows up.

This is a picture of the devil. The birds of the air come immediately after the Word is sown. Every time you make a sacrifice, the enemy will be there to try to get you to take off the altar what you've placed on the altar. Abraham has to defend what he has placed on the altar. The birds of the air are coming from every direction, and he's driving them away persistently. There are times when we have to drive away all the distractions, temptations, doubts, and fears that the enemy tries to bring into our life. We've got to take the sword of the Spirit and wield it.

Abraham's story continues. "The sun was going down," and as the sun was going down, something happened to Abraham. The Bible says, "*A deep sleep fell upon Abram; and behold, terror and great darkness fell upon him*" (Gen. 15:12). Terror and great darkness. I believe the terror was associated with the birds of prey. As long as there is daylight, you can see where they're coming from, and you've got a chance of defeating them; but as the sun goes down, you lack vision, you lack clarity. It's getting darker and darker, and in the midst of that darkness you think, *Can things get any worse than this?* Some of you have been there.

The fear that you have is a fear of great darkness. "Lord, if the sun sets, I'm in trouble. I won't be able to know where all these attacks are coming from. I can't see. I've got a lack of vision." There are times when God will allow us to face these situations where we lack vision, or we lack understanding. It seems to be a time of darkness, and we become fearful. Can it become any worse than it is?

Genesis 15:17 says, "*It came about when the sun had set, that it was **very** dark.*" So the thing that Abraham fears the most comes upon him. When it is very dark outside, *you can't see the stars.* Oh when there are no clouds and the night is clear you can travel out into the country and see the stars without any problem. In fact the Bible says, "The stars were given as lights" (see Gen. 1:14-15). You can walk home by the light of the moon; it can be so bright some nights, especially out in the country, that you can walk home without any problem at all. But when there is a cloud cover, you look up, and you cannot see a single star; all is total darkness. It's then when those promises seem to be so far away that you need to persist—holding onto God's Word regardless of feelings or "sight."

Prior to this, anytime Abraham doubted or became discouraged, all he had to do was look into the heaven, and there night after night, he was reminded of God's promise that his seed would be as the stars of Heaven. Now, however, he can't begin to envision the promises due to the darkness. Likewise, there are seasons like that in our Christian life, when that prophetic word, that word that you've been holding onto for months or years—it has kept you going—but now somehow it's lost its reality, so to speak, and you find yourself in a place of absolute darkness.

Yet it was in that place of extreme darkness that the Lord finally appeared to Abraham. What I'm trying to convey is that there are seasons; every man or woman of God has those seasons. We see also in the life of men like Moses, his season on the backside of the desert, no doubt preparation for his shepherding of a million of God's cantankerous sheep through their 40-year wilderness.

Survive the Wilderness Season

I recall vividly after leaving New Zealand in 1988 my own personal wilderness. We had been part of a large wonderful church for 15 years. We were secure, loved, and accepted by the people. Our children were attending a great Christian school; one was already in college. We were settled into a comfortable home and had everything we needed when I felt the Lord leading us to return to the States. Talk about a step of faith. I was determined to live by the principle that God was sufficient to meet all my needs and that He alone was going to have to open doors and supply our needs. I've never in 40 years of ministry asked for a meeting or put out a newsletter asking for support, and yet I can honestly say that God has more than abundantly provided for my family and me. We arrived in Dallas, Texas, bought a home there, fully believing that God would open doors for my ministry. However, very few doors opened that year. Months went by with hardly any meetings, and needless to say I spent a lot of time in prayer.

During a rather tenuous time, my wife came to me. As you know, many wives have a tendency to want to nest; they want to settle; they want to have that security of knowing that everything is OK. She came to me saying, "David, have we made a mistake?"

And I remember that out of my mouth came these words—I'm not sure where they came from—but I said, "Darling, don't deprive me of my wilderness." Upon moving to Dallas, all of a sudden everything had been stripped from me. The team of men that I had worked so closely with was now gone. I was all alone; no doors were opening; but I was alone with God. Day after day, I pored over His Word, and God began to reveal new truths to me. It was a season I wouldn't want to go through again, but neither would I trade it for anything.

Joseph, too, went through his own wilderness. He had the promise, but it took some 13 years before he saw the fulfillment of that promise. I tell people that there is a difference between the *call* of God and the *commission* of God. We see the call of God as Jesus challenged His disciples at the beginning of His ministry to forsake everything and follow Him—that was their call. The commission came three years later, *"Go into all the world and preach the gospel"* (Mark 16:15). In between the call and the commission, there is always preparation.

Returning to Joseph's life, he had the call. The call was, "I'm going to raise you up. Men are going to bow down before you. Your own family is going to bow down before you." But between the call and the commission there were 13 years of preparation, 13 years of hardship, disappointment, rejection, and accusations. The Bible says that God put him in prison, and he was in irons, he was afflicted, until the Word of God came to pass. It's all part of being a well-seasoned man or woman of God.

Persistency Leads to Maturity

I'm trying to drive home this point to make you understand: Don't be fearful of going through these seasons. Understand them. They are part of God's purpose and process, and if we handle them correctly they can make us mature men and women of God. It isn't always easy going; God never said it would be. The Word of God never conveys that. I know we've have certain doctrines floating around in the church that teach that if you confess loudly enough, you can escape all these things. But certainly this is not "sound doctrine," not biblical, and nobody I know in the Bible ever did it. We don't have Jeremiah confessing that he won't end up in a pit, nor do we have Joseph confessing that he won't end up in prison. No, it's all part of this process that God will take us through.

We have to battle sometimes against discouragement, fears, insecurity, and loneliness. I can still hear my friend Peter Morrow sharing an illustration in which the devil was having an auction, getting rid of some of the old equipment that was now worn and outdated. The demons were helping him by running around picking up old instruments that they were going to auction off. Soon one of them came with a very worn-out instrument and said, "Here, devil, this looks like it's pretty well worn out. Shall we put this up for auction?"

The devil instantly responded, "No, no, no, no. Whatever you do, don't ever, ever, ever touch that. That's my most valuable instrument. The reason it's so worn is that I've used it and used it."

Surprised, the demon asked, "What is it?"

"Discouragement," said the devil.

There are times when we become overwhelmed with discouragement. We think the whole world has turned against us and there is no way out. What we need to do during times like that is to heed the writer of Hebrews, when he says, *"Looking unto Jesus, the author and finisher of our faith"* (Heb. 12:2 NKJV).

Surviving the anointing requires PERSISTENCY. Don't give up!

Chapter 5

Purity

Of itself purity is not power, but it clears the way.

—T. Henry Howard

The detached life is the result of an intensely narrow moral purity, not of a narrow mind. The mental view of Jesus Christ was as big as God's view, consequently He went anywhere—to marriage feasts, into the social life of His time, because His morality was absolutely pure; and that is what God wants of us.

—Oswald Chambers

IN this chapter we want to look at the absolute necessity of Purity. This is a "non- negotiable." In the introduction I mentioned that there are 1,500 ministers a month falling. The primary reason is sexual uncleanness of some type. We now have, according to the latest statistics, somewhere in the realm of 25 million web sites devoted exclusively to pornography—25 million! Talk about spiritual land mines. Every time you log onto the Internet you're within a mouse click of one of the most deadly devices the devil has ever concocted. Just one brief glance is enough to snag you and propel you into a life of bondage and heartache. Porn is the devil's "superglue"; just one touch and you can't break free from it. The statistics alone are proof of that.

Several years ago I was holding some meetings in the Midwestern United States. The senior pastor was also the overseer for his region, which happened to be a part of a Pentecostal denomination. As we were sharing together he remarked that they currently had a need for 19 pastors to replace 19 who had fallen due to some type of sexual sin.

According to a survey by Promise Keepers, 65 percent of the men surveyed said they struggled with some form of sexual addiction—65 percent! Unlike any other generation in history we are being bombarded with sexual slime from every direction. It's almost impossible to pick up a book or magazine or turn on the radio or television without seeing or hearing some type of sexually explicit material been shown, written, or talked about. The enemy has taken this very beautiful, precious, and holy area intended by God for the pleasure of a husband and wife and has twisted, distorted, and violated it.

There may be some women reading this and thinking to themselves, "I know that's a major problem that men have." You may be surprised to hear that according to a recent Oprah Winfrey show, Americans spend around $57 billion a year on pornography— some $20 billion in child pornography alone. It's one of the largest industries in the world. But what was the most revealing: "The largest consumers of pornography in America are women and not men." Women become deeply involved in romance novels; they follow all the "soaps" on the afternoon television shows. Oprah classifies that (and I would too) as pornography.

Every one of us has to face this unrelenting attack. Therefore we have to know how to guard our lives. I was recently talking to a mailman who had some 1,100 stops on his daily route. He estimated that about 10 percent of the mail he delivered included some form of pornographic material. What can we do?

God's Word makes clear that we are to flee youthful lusts. We are told that the will of God for us is to abstain from sexual immorality. It takes effort and determination in order to do that.

The Assemblies of God, the largest Pentecostal denomination in America, sent out a letter five or six years ago to Assembly of God pastors, warning them about one thing: the danger of pornography on the Internet. These were ministers. The letter was never intended for the congregation, not that they couldn't see it or know about it necessarily, but it was specifically sent out from Springfield, Missouri, to warn pastors—because so many leaders have fallen in this particular area.

Develop a Hatred of Sin

In order to guard ourselves, we need the fear of God in our lives, don't we? The fear of God, which is to hate evil, is one teaching that is missing in the church at large today. When you fear something, you avoid it. If I fear heights, then you won't find me looking down from a 30-story building. If I have a fear of heights, I'm going to be as far away from that edge as I can possibly get. Likewise the fear of the Lord is to hate evil. If you hate something, there is no longer any real temptation. If you hate chocolate ice cream (not too many people do), and you're faced with a choice, you're not even going to be tempted by it because you hate it. So it makes sense that what you fear, or what you hate, is not really a temptation. That's why the Bible says, *"The fear of the Lord is the beginning of wisdom"* (Prov. 1:7). The fear of the Lord is to hate evil.

We need the fear of God to come into the church, to give us a hatred for sin. Too many people know that sin is wrong—we all know that—but we don't hate it. I've asked God many, many times, "Lord, give me a hatred for sin." It's one of the greatest keys to surviving the anointing.

I can remember back to the time when I was a young minister. My wife and I, along with our first child who was only three months old, were sailing from New York City to New Zealand. After arriving, we moved into a small house on a little island off the coast of New Zealand, called The Great Barrier Island. The gentleman we worked with at that time was a wonderful godly man who held a conference on the island every year for any believers who wanted to come. My wife and I had been instrumental in introducing Youth With A Mission (YWAM) to New Zealand at that time, and Loren Cunningham, the international director of YWAM, was there as a guest speaker along with some other local men and women of God. The conference organizers pitched a large tent for the meetings, and people started to arrive from all over the region.

At that conference, the message that made the greatest impact on my life was given by a great man of God named Milton Smith. He spoke on the "fear of the Lord" for an entire hour. At the end of the message, I remember asking some of the leaders if they would pray over me. Joy Dawson was one of those people, along with some others, who joined me in a small office only some six feet by ten. I knelt down and asked if they would lay their hands on me and pray that the Lord would place the fear of God on my life.

You see, I knew that sin was wrong, but I didn't fear it, and over the years I've asked God to continue to place His fear in my life. I think the best way I can explain the fear of God is like this. When I was a student in high school I was subjected to every temptation like everybody else. We had just moved from England to America as a family, and I was 15 years old at the time. There was every opportunity to be involved in sin, sexual activities, drinking, smoking, plus a hundred other things. Drugs weren't very prevalent in those days, but everything else was, and I was tempted like anybody else. But I knew one thing: If I got involved in any of those things, and my father found out about it, that I would devastate my father. I knew everything my father stood and lived for, his message of holiness, his emphasis on prayer and knowing God. I knew that if I became involved in any of these things, and my father found out that I was smoking or drinking or sleeping around, it would literally break his heart and destroy his life.

Even though I was tempted to do those things, I had such a regard, such a love, for my father, I held him in such high honor and esteem, that I did not want to hurt my father. So basically, the thing that kept me safe through those years of high school was my love for my father. That's what the fear of God is: It's the love for a greater Father, an understanding of who He is and what He represents, His nature, His character, His holiness, and the knowledge that when we sin, we break the heart of God.

God is looking for a holy people. The message prior to the first coming of the Lord Jesus Christ was a message of repentance, and I believe the message that will precede the second coming is also a message of repentance, *"Prepare ye the way of the Lord"* (Luke 3:4 KJV). The Bible emphatically declares that without holiness *"no one will see the Lord"* (Heb. 12:14).

One evening during the "Pensacola revival," there was a large number who responded to the invitation. I was sitting on the platform and was asked if I could assist with those who had come forward. I randomly went towards a man and said, "Can I pray with you?"

And he said, "Yes."

I asked, "Is there any specific area I could pray with you about?"

"Yes," he said and then told me that he too was a preacher. "I travel around the world preaching the faith message. I'm a faith preacher." He continued, "I was sitting in the meeting tonight as Steve Hill was preaching. God spoke to me and said, 'Without faith it's impossible to please Me.' But then I heard Him say, 'Without holiness no man will see Me.' I have some unfinished business that needs to be taken care of." Later he told me, "I realize that while faith is important, holiness is essential."

Holiness Is Essential

We have many, many exhortations regarding holiness in the Word of God. Isaiah 52:11 says, *"Be clean, you who bear the vessels of the Lord"* (Isa. 52:11 NKJV). **Be clean.** It's talking about the priests; it's talking about those who functioned in the tabernacle, their handling of the holy vessels, but we can obviously take that to the New Testament and apply it just as equally. Paul said to Timothy, *"If a man therefore purge himself from these, he shall be a vessel unto honour, sanctified, and meet for the master's use"* (2 Tim. 2:21 KJV). God looks for clean vessels; He's looking for a clean Church, a Church without spot and without wrinkle. In the Old Testament, spots and wrinkles spoke of blemishes and defects, and God is looking for a Church that is without blemish and without defect.

Holiness is best defined as spiritual health. In America we spend literally billions of dollars a year on health-related products, whether it's exercising equipment, tennis shoes, or popping vitamin pills. Why? Because we want to maintain healthy bodies. We take it seriously. We do our exercises routinely; all because of "health." Now the moment we get a twinge of pain we are off to the doctor; we want that thing diagnosed; we want the doctor to tell us what's wrong. The sooner we are able to see the doctor, the quicker we can begin the necessary treatment.

We don't like living with pain because we know that it's indicative that something is wrong. At the first sign of pain we contact the doctor's office to make an appointment. If the receptionist at the doctor's office says he's busy and can't see you until Friday, we usually respond by saying, "If there's a cancellation, please call me." We want that appointment as soon as possible. We want the pain dealt with; we don't want to have to wait a week to find out the root cause. And yet, when it comes to the sickness of sin, we can go for years and never go to the Great Physician for help.

Holiness means that we can look God in the face, so to speak, and know that we don't have to drop our head in shame. As the old hymn says, "Nothing between my soul and the Savior." We can thank God that the blood of Jesus Christ, God's Son, makes that possible. And yet, there is also a part that you and I play in that process: We have to keep ourselves clean. Paul says, *"If a man purge **himself** from these things"* (see 2 Tim. 2:21).

Now you may say, "Well, I came from a Catholic background, and that sounds to me like a 'works' salvation." No, we are not saved by works, but there is a sense in which we do have a part to play in maintaining our walk. The best way I can illustrate this is by taking you back to the feasts of Israel. The very first feast was the feast of Passover. This began by the children of Israel's slaying a lamb for each household. After draining the blood from the lamb, they would take hyssop and dip it into the blood, then proceed to sprinkle the blood on the doorposts and lintel of their home. The blood was never sprinkled on the floor, as that would signify the trampling underfoot of the greater lamb, the Lamb of God. God revealed to Moses, *"When I see the blood I will pass over you"* (Exod. 12:13).

The Israelites were redeemed by the blood of the Lamb. There was nothing that they could do to gain the slightest merit. It was simply on the basis of the shed blood of the lamb—although they did have to obey God's instructions. That's the way you and I are saved, by grace and by grace alone, but that doesn't mean that we sit back and do nothing.

The moment Passover ended, another feast began: the feast of Unleavened Bread. In this feast, every Israelite was responsible for removing any trace of leaven from their dwelling. They had to open every drawer, cupboard, canister, and so on, and if they found any trace of leaven, they had to remove it. That's what we see in the New Testament as well. We are redeemed by grace, redeemed by the blood of the Lamb, but we have to maintain by obedience to the Word of God in our daily walk. Paul tells us how he lived, *"I exercise myself daily,"* *"I buffet my body,"* *"to have always a conscience void to offence toward God, and toward man"* (Acts 24:16 KJV). Little wonder then that Paul passes on to Timothy this same urgent exhortation: *"Purge yourself from these things; if you do this, you will be a vessel unto honour, sanctified, and meet for the master's use"* (see 2 Tim. 2:21 KJV).

I like to think of it as "spiritual maintenance." God doesn't come down to read us His Word every day and then lead us in prayer. We've got to do those things for ourselves. As we read the Word of God, it acts as a mirror, revealing to us those areas of our life that need to be cleansed. It is then our responsibility to confess those needs to God and ask for cleansing. A mirror in the natural shows us our physical condition, but it cannot change us. We have to take charge of what the mirror reveals. If the mirror reveals that our hair is messy, our clothes are dirty, or we are too fat, then we are the ones who have to take action.

Purity is so vitally important. The house of God is to be a "separated" house. *"Come out from among them, and be ye separate, saith the Lord"* (2 Cor. 6:17 KJV). In the Old Testament, in First Chronicles chapter 21, David has sinned against God, so God sent a sword against the nation of Israel and 70,000 people died. As David is offering his sacrifices there on the threshing floor of Ornan the Jebusite, all of a sudden he has a revelation. He says, "This is the house of God." It was on that very threshing floor that Solomon later built the temple.

What is the significance of a threshing floor? A threshing floor is a place of separation. Threshing floors are interesting, and it is an interesting study in the Word of God to look at threshing floors. It was at the threshing floor that Ruth approached Boaz. Threshing floors in the life of David are interesting as well. It was at a threshing floor that the oxen nearly upset the ark of the covenant and a man died, which led to David's seeking God and inquiring of Him the reason. In Luke 3:17 we read: *"His winnowing fork is in His hand to thoroughly clear His threshing floor, and to gather the wheat into His barn; but He will burn up the chaff with unquenchable fire."*

God is calling His Church to be a separated people, called out from the world. The world is to be crucified to us; we are to be crucified to the world. It is absolutely imperative that we begin to see the message of holiness restored to the Church. By "holiness" I'm not just referring to a standard of dress, but that inner desire to walk circumspectly in the fear of the Lord. The modern Church in its desire to see results has largely minimized the message of separation and sanctification. Recently a friend of mine who attends one of the nation's largest churches began dating after a failed marriage. He was shocked and saddened to find that almost all the women he dated were more interested in going to bed with him than in anything else. This is the result of emphasizing self above the Savior.

Think about the time when David sinned by taking another man's wife: Bathsheba. Later he was confronted by the prophet Nathan, who summarized David's actions by telling him a story. The story Nathan told was of a rich man with a large number of sheep, and a poor man with only one little lamb. A traveler came to the rich man, and the end result was that in order to satisfy the needs of the traveler, the rich man stole from the poor man the only sheep he had. Of course we know that the rich man in the story symbolized David, and the poor man's only lamb symbolized Bathsheba.

I recall an old man of God saying to me while I was still a young man, "David, beware of 'travelers.'" What he meant was that "travelers" are thoughts or temptations that come knocking at the door of our minds. How we respond to them determines whether we live with a pure and undefiled conscience before God or not. The Book of Proverbs has many warnings along these lines. One is the picture of the fool who takes the path to the house of the harlot, not realizing that *"many...have been slain"* (Prov. 7:26 KJV) by doing that very thing.

When Jesus taught His disciples, He made it clear to them, *"If your right eye makes you stumble, tear it out, throw it from you; for it is better for you to lose one of the parts of your body, than for your whole body to be thrown into hell"* (Matt. 5:29).

Let's look at Matthew 5:27-30, *"You have heard that it was said, 'You shall not commit adultery'; but I say to you that everyone who looks at a woman with lust for her has already committed adultery with her in his heart. ...If your right hand makes you stumble, cut it off."* What was Jesus referring to here? The *hand* is used to physically satisfy what the *eye* stirs up by lust. Through the eye comes stimulation; through the hand comes participation or action. The hand is used for masturbation and other such things. You see the whole context here is speaking about sexual sin. I'm being very clear, very explicit, because it needs to be said. Paul warns the Corinthians not to be deceived into thinking that if they are practicing sexual sin that they can still enter into God's Kingdom.

Finally we see in the closing chapter of the Book of Revelation, one final warning: *"Let the one...who is filthy, still be filthy; and let the one who is righteous, still practice righteousness; and the one who is holy, still keep **himself** holy"* (Rev. 22:11).

Chapter 6

Empathy/ Compassion

Except I be moved with compassion,
How dwelleth Thy Spirit in me?
In word and in deed
Burning love is my need:
I know I can find this in Thee.

—Albert Orsborn, *Salvation Army Song Book*

William Booth, founder of the Salvation Army, stated:

While women weep as they do now, I'll fight; while little children go hungry, as they do now I'll fight; while men go to prison, in and out, in and out, as they do now, I'll fight; while there is a drunkard left, while there is a poor lost girl upon the streets, while there remains one dark soul without the light of God, I'll fight—I'll fight to the very end![1]

I fully believe that another key to surviving the anointing of the Spirit of God is to maintain that softness, gentleness, and tenderness that can only come as we become intimately acquainted with the Spirit of God. We must continually allow His compassion, mercy, and love to flow forth through us. Once again we have the example of Jesus, the pattern Son. We read in Matthew 9:36 (NKJV), *"When He saw the multitudes, He was moved with compassion."* And in Luke 19:41 (KJV) it says that when Jesus *"beheld the city,"* He *"wept over it."*

In other words, Jesus was a man who could identify with the needs of others. He could weep with those who wept, He could laugh with those who laughed, and He was able to understand what people were going through. Once we lose that sense of compassion or ability to empathize we gradually become "professionals," knowing what to do but no longer doing it out of a heart of compassion but rather as an obligation to our calling.

The Heart of a Shepherd

I believe the difference between a shepherd and a hireling is that one has a genuine love for the sheep; the other simply does the job because there is a paycheck at the end of the week. Personally, I don't want to ever become professional and lose that shepherd's heart. I want to be able to cry and weep as Jesus wept, or better yet, allow Jesus to cry and weep through me. If, after a period of time goes by, in my own devotional life I'm no longer able to weep or be moved with compassion, then I should be concerned with the state of my own heart. Jesus wept over Jerusalem, and I believe He still weeps. I believe that He weeps over your city and mine, over your nation and mine. He weeps over the nations that are still in bondage to the powers of darkness.

The Church has largely become indifferent to the world around it. We no longer see men and women as sheep having no shepherd; we simply see them through our natural eyes, as professionals, dressed up and going to their respective offices and workplaces, but we don't see beyond that. Jesus saw beyond what was just the outward appearance, and He saw a lost generation, a generation that had no guidance, a generation that had nobody to care for them, nobody to bind up their wounds, pour in the oil and the wine, so to speak.

One of the things that Jesus reprimanded the Pharisees over was the fact that they were meticulous when it came to keeping certain elements of the law, like tithing, fasting, and the like, but when it came to the "weightier matters," they failed miserably. They had little if any compassion towards their fellowmen. Jesus pleads with them, saying, *"Go and learn what this means: 'I desire compassion, and not sacrifice'"* (Matt. 9:13). He went on. *"You load people down with heavy burdens; you're not there to help them; you're not there to lift them"* (see Luke 11:46). They had become hard, cruel taskmasters, lording it over God's people. Once we allow that religious type of professionalism to come into our lives, we might as well retire from the ministry—or we should repent.

Time after time we read in the Word of God how the prophets would reprimand the shepherds because of their attitude toward the sheep, because of their insensitivity, how they failed to bind up those who were broken or help those who were diseased. They simply used the flock to gratify and satisfy their own needs. Jesus said, *"The good shepherd lays down His life for the sheep"* (John 10:11). *Lord, please grant us some true shepherds.*

We need to marinate ourselves in the love of God until we become tender, compassionate, kind, gracious, and loving. When

God replaced King Saul, He did so with a man who had the smell of sheep all over him. If you don't love "sheep," forget about the ministry. If you continue, you will only produce problems both for the flock and also for yourself at the judgment seat of Christ.

I love this portion of Scripture in First Thessalonians 2 where Paul lays bare his heart. He tells the Church that he could have come wielding a heavy hand of "apostolic" authority over them, but instead he chose to be gentle, like a mother holding a newborn. He expressed his deep love for them by telling them he didn't come simply as a preacher but as one willing to give his life to them. He shared with them that in order not to be a burden to them, he worked, so he could prove that his motivation was not based on greed. Wow! Would to God we had some "apostles" like that today who, instead of having to constantly beg for support, would get a job.

In another place Paul states, *"I was 'serving the Lord...with tears'"* (Acts 20:19). Paul was able to break down with emotion as he saw the needs in the Body. He wept out of his deep love and compassion.

God wants to birth in us compassion—compassion for the lost, compassion for the suffering, compassion for those who are in bondage, compassion for those less fortunate than ourselves. When our eyes are dry, so is our heart.

"Try Tears"

My father would often relate the story of William Booth. During the height of the Salvation Army, that wonderful organization began to spread out and literally take over the world of its day—truly one of the great missionary movements of our time. Several ladies had gone out to serve in a particular region, only to find out that they were running into obstacle after obstacle. The people were indifferent, their message was not being received, and they had tried everything they could. They were finally at their wits' end, not knowing where to go next or what to do next. They felt like they had given and done everything they could, but there was very little fruit to show for their effort.

In desperation, they sent a telegram to William Booth, explaining, "We've tried everything. What should we do now?"

William Booth sent a telegram back. It had two words on it: "Try tears."

Try tears. When all else fails, try tears. Allow God to break you.

I think one of the most beautiful statements that Paul ever made is recorded there in Second Timothy 1:4, where Paul is expressing his desire to see Timothy: *"Longing to see you, even as I recall your tears, so that I may be filled with joy."*

But put yourself in Timothy's place. Imagine that you are the understudy or apprentice to a great man of God. You have been mentored by this man. He's famous, and he writes a letter, and that letter makes its way onto the Internet (if I can modernize this a little). Now the entire world can read this very personal letter where your friend writes, "I recall your tears." You would not think that was much of a compliment. In fact, you'd probably say, "Boy, I wish he hadn't put that in there. It makes me look like a big 'cry baby.' I wish he would have written something like, 'I recall your great preaching. I recall your great teaching. I recall your great intercession. I recall your great signs, wonders, and miracles'—now that would have made my day."

This though is the greatest compliment Paul ever wrote to anybody: "I recall your tears." In other words Paul is saying, "Timothy, when I think of you, I think of a compassionate man— one so sensitive to the Spirit of God that you are able to be broken over the things that break the heart of God." As Paul and

Timothy traveled around on these missionary journeys, they would come into a city or town and Timothy would sense the longing on the heart of God for the region. Paul would take notice of this young man as he broke in the presence of God. He would see the tears flow as Timothy began to lift that burden back to God in prayer. Little wonder then that Paul writes, "Timothy, I miss you, and I miss your tears." What a beautiful picture.

That's what God wants us to have. Yet we can become so callous, can't we? So indifferent, so insensitive to the needs of others that we just see them numerically—we treat them as just another number. God is longing to give us the heart of a shepherd: His heart. Without His compassion we will ultimately grieve the Spirit and lose the precious anointing that works through compassion.

Jesus was anointed with the Spirit of God. He saw through the eyes of the Spirit. If we are not seeing that way, then we need to say, "Lord, there was a time when I used to break. There was a time when I was sensitive to the needs of others. But somehow I've lost that. Please restore in me a heart like Yours."

Maybe you're a cell group leader, youth pastor, worship leader, etc., and it's just become part of a job, a routine, a ritual. You no longer take it seriously; you've lost your heart for the sheep. If that's true, then you need to ask the Lord to once again restore to you His heart for His people.

Pharaohs Versus Fathers

Hardly a month goes by that I don't receive a call or e-mail from someone wanting to be "heard." They are looking for a father, someone who will take the time to listen to them and give them some fatherly advice or encouragement. One young man came to see me recently and shared how he and his wife felt called to a major city on the East Coast. This young man led a very large youth group. He was so successful that other youth pastors came to him to learn all they could from him. When he approached his pastor and shared his burden, his pastor told him he would make the "call" as he was "the pastor." Needless to say, the pastor did not want to lose this gifted young couple and so chose to use the authority card to control them. He eventually released them but told them he would never have anything to do with them—from that moment on they were on their own.

How tragic. I call that type of leader a Pharaoh not a father. I'm grateful to God that He allowed me to be raised by spiritual fathers—men who never wielded the authority card at me but who sought to influence me through example, persuasion, and prayer. One of my spiritual fathers would say to me if someone decided to leave the church, "I'm not sure they are making the right decision, but I want to bless them regardless; that way they will always feel welcome to come back if things don't work out."

I can hear some of you saying to yourself, "This guy doesn't believe in 'covering.'" Yes I do, but I believe there is a vast difference between being a Pharaoh and a father. Here is the difference.

PHARAOHS	FATHERS
Pharaohs have slaves.	Fathers have sons.
Pharaohs command.	Fathers counsel.
Pharaohs dominate.	Fathers liberate.
Pharaohs dictate.	Fathers communicate.
Pharaohs destroy and demean.	Fathers discipline.
Pharaohs remove.	Fathers restore.
Pharaohs restrain.	Fathers release.

Pharaohs manipulate.	Fathers motivate.
Pharaohs emasculate.	Fathers propagate.
Pharaohs whip.	Fathers weep.
Pharaohs want results.	Fathers want relationship.
Pharaohs build great cities.	Fathers build great sons.
Pharaohs are hardhearted.	Fathers are tenderhearted.
Pharaohs fear success.	Fathers foster success.
Pharaohs want servants.	Fathers are servants.
Pharaohs prey on slaves.	Fathers pray for sons.
Slaves die for pharaohs.	Fathers die for sons.
Slaves work out of fear.	Sons work out of faith.
Slaves work out of duty.	Sons work out of devotion.
Slaves remain slaves.	Sons develop into fathers.
Slaves loathe pharaohs.	Sons love fathers.
Slaves are discouraged.	Sons are encouraged.
Slaves receive reproof.	Sons receive approval.
Slaves grow to hate and hurt.	Sons grow to heal and help.
Slaves have numbers.	Sons have names.
Slaves celebrate a pharaoh's death.	Sons commiserate a father's death.
Slaves escape.	Sons return.
Slaves sigh.	Sons sing.

Endnote

1. William Booth, as quoted in J. Evan Smith's *Booth the Beloved* (Oxford University Press, 1949), 123-124.

Chapter 7

Humility

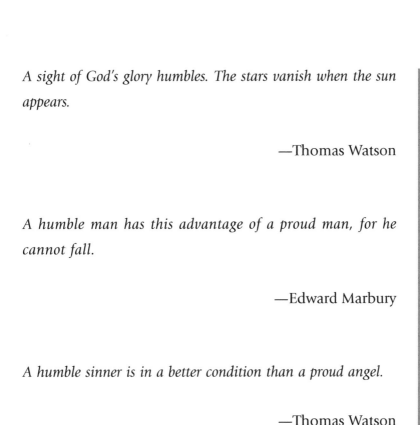

A sight of God's glory humbles. The stars vanish when the sun appears.

—Thomas Watson

A humble man has this advantage of a proud man, for he cannot fall.

—Edward Marbury

A humble sinner is in a better condition than a proud angel.

—Thomas Watson

God's choice acquaintances are humble men.

—Robert Leighton

UMILITY. Surely there is no greater need in the Body of Christ today than for truly humble men and women of God. The Puritans used to say, "Pride is the *last* thing that leaves the human heart, and the *first* thing that returns." Let me say that again, "Pride is the last thing to leave the human heart and the first thing to return."

As we consider Jesus as our "pattern Son," notice His appeal to those who would follow Him. *"Come unto Me, all ye that labour and are heavy laden, and I will give you rest. Take My yoke upon you, and learn of Me; for I am **meek** and **lowly**...and ye shall find rest unto your souls"* (Matt. 11:28-29 KJV). One thing about Jesus: He was a humble man. His nature is one of humility. The word "humble" comes from the Latin word humus, and if you know anything about Latin (I studied it for three years, believe it or not, but I can't remember a single thing), *humus* means earthy, dirt, down to earth. There is something about people who are "down to earth." They are free from that sense of superiority and eliteness. You feel drawn to them rather than repelled.

Why is humility so vital? First of all because it is a hallmark of God's divine nature. Another good reason is that apart from it you will find yourself being opposed by God. For God *"resists the proud, but gives grace to the humble"* (James 4:6 NKJV).

God Resists the Proud

Some of you may have heard the name "Francis Frangipane." Or maybe you've read some of his books. He is a wonderful teacher, a wonderful man of God. Francis has a strong emphasis on intercession, spiritual warfare, but would refuse to go to a city unless the churches cooperated together—he believed in unity. Due to his emphasis on spiritual warfare, he would often be asked if he had sensed anything about the city he was in. Intercessors, of course, have always got their antennas up, listening for what God may reveal to them.

They would ask Francis, "Are you sensing anything? We know we're up against some sort of principality that seems to be hindering what God wants to do here." Francis would say, almost with a twinkle in his eye, "Yes, I know what you're up against." Then they were riveted, listening intently.

"Really, you mean you know the principality?"

"Yes, I know the principality," Francis would say.

"Wow! Well, what is it? Do you know the name?"

"Yeah, I know the name of the principality."

By then they were usually very impressed, and they'd say, "Well, tell us, what's the name?"

He would look at them and say, "The principality you're up against is Yahweh."

They would look at him and say, "Yahweh? Did you say *Yahweh*?"

"Yes, I said Yahweh."

"But that's God's name."

"Yes I know. God is the one who is resisting you."

"But that doesn't make sense."

"Oh it makes perfect sense to me," Francis would explain. "Ever since I've been with your group, you've talked about how great you are; you've talked about how great your denomination is; how great this is and that is. You tend to look down your nose at others and their work. You've allowed pride to come into your life as a group, as a denomination, as a movement. You feel superior; you feel you've got greater insight and greater revelation. You really feel a little more superior to others." He would go on to remind them that *"God resists the proud"* (James 4:6 NKJV).

Pride—the Root of All Sin

There is this growing tendency within all of us, whether corporately or individually, to allow over a period of time, a sense of being a little better than everybody else—a little better educated, a little more spiritual or sacrificial, or one of any number of other things. However, if we're going to know the grace and the enabling power of God in our life, we need to heed what the Bible says, *"He has shown you, O man, what is good; and what does the Lord require of you but to do justly, to love mercy, and to walk humbly with your God?"* (Mic. 6:8 NKJV).

Pride is a terrible thing. It's the root of all sin. Yet it's one of those sins that we sometimes become accustomed to. Often we fail to recognize it or we simply overlook it. We turn on the television, maybe the evening news, and it's talking about a serial killer or rapist and we think, *How terrible.* We are shocked and revolted at the thought. But when have you ever turned on the evening news and heard that some well-known dignitary had become proud? We're conditioned to the fact that certain sins are considered vile while other sins are normal and even acceptable.

Years ago while still living and ministering in New Zealand, I walked into our church's bookstore and immediately had a book thrust into my hand by the store manager, Bruce. "David," he said, "You have to read this. You'll enjoy it." The book was open to a chapter dealing with David's greatest sin. When we talk about David's greatest sin, most of us immediately think about his sin with Bathsheba. Hollywood has made movies about it; the world knows about it. Everybody knows about David's sin with Bathsheba. As a result of that sin, Bathsheba lost their baby; it lived for just a brief period of time before God took it.

However, this was not the greatest sin in David's life. One day while David was sitting in his house, the enemy came and began to incite him into thinking about his own great power and might. Soon David became intoxicated with pride as he tried to imagine all those under his authority. Within minutes he had summoned Joab to take a census throughout the land of Israel.

Joab immediately realizes what David is thinking and pleads with him to stop. David refuses to listen, and Joab is forced to carry out the order he's been given. Nine months later Joab returns with the information David is seeking. Joab informs David that he has over a million and a half men who are able to pick up the sword.

David was not interested in the type of census that God told Moses to take, but rather he had requested a specific census that would determine how powerful he was militarily. David had succumbed to the wiles of the enemy by taking his eyes off the Lord and His strength, and looking instead to his own. Barely were the words out of Joab's mouth when David sees the immensity of his sin. "I have sinned exceedingly," he says. God is angry at what David has done and sends the prophet Gad to give him the word as to what is going to happen. Gad gives David three choices. David chooses to fall into the merciful hands of God—the end result being that David loses 70,000 men.

I will never forget the day that I came to realize that David's sin of *passion* cost him one life, but his sin of *pride* cost him

70,000 lives! Pride is a terrible and hideous sin. We need to remain humble in the sight of the Lord. Somebody once said, "You can't humble yourself," but I disagree. The Bible says that you can humble yourself; you *"humble yourself in the sight of Lord"* (James 4:10 NKJV). You see, pride flourishes when we take our eyes off the Lord.

Let's suppose that I can play the piano and I think I'm pretty good. I've had five or six years of lessons and feel quite confident in my ability. One day as I'm playing, in walks a world-renowned, classical pianist. As soon as I finish, he sits down at the piano and plays some difficult piece flawlessly. It doesn't take long for me to understand how insignificant I am in comparison to him.

That's the way we humble ourselves, by turning our gaze upon the One who created the heavens and the earth, the One who calls the stars by name, the One who sits above the vault of the earth and reduces rulers to nothing. It's rather difficult to think of yourself as important in view of God's greatness, isn't it?

Madame Guyon is by far one of the best known women in Church history. In the book *Spiritual Writings*, she gives her insights into various passages in Genesis. *"Now in those days there were giants upon the earth. For the sons of God having taken to wife the daughters of men, their children became the mightiest of the age and men of renown"* (see Gen. 6:4). Guyon's comments on that passage are as follows:

> *The giants and monsters of pride come only from the mixing of the human and the divine. All the great men of renown in the world have been those who made fleshly wisdom triumph, concealed under a little spirituality. Oh the frightful monster! You will see persons puffed up and elevated like **giants** by the estimation that they have of themselves, on account of their natural talents accompanied by some spiritual maxims: and who nevertheless are buried in nature, and in the secret esteem of*

their own conduct. They are, however, the extraordinary men, and of great reputation. But as for those who by dint of self-renunciation have become wholly annihilated, as for them I say, they are unknown: they are not even distinguished from other men. And how would they be distinguished amongst those **giants**, *since they are so little, that they appear when near them only as ants, which they tread underfoot with contempt, and regard often as useless things upon the earth? But, oh God, Thou "who resisteth the proud and giveth grace to the humble," Thou sheddest it abundantly on these little valleys fitted to contain it, while these pompous and superb mountains cannot receive a drop without allowing it to flow down upon these little ones, who acknowledge themselves so much the more unworthy of it, the more they are filled with it.*[1]

In Luke chapter 10, we have the disciples coming back at the end of a day of ministry, and they're excited. They're excited for this reason: They had seen numerous people delivered from demonic possession. Luke 10:17 says, *"The seventy returned with joy, saying, 'Lord even the demons are subject to us in Your name.'"* I imagine that was a great day for those disciples; they'd been watching Jesus cast out demons on a regular basis and now they had been given the authority to cast them out also. They arrived back at the end of the day and couldn't wait to tell the Lord the good news, "Lord, even the demons are subject to *us* in Your name" (see Luke 10:17). Basically they were saying, "Lord, we've had a 'blast' today. It was terrific. You wouldn't believe the number of devils we cast out."

Jesus looks at them and responds, *"I was watching satan fall from heaven like lightning. Behold, I have given you authority to tread on serpents and scorpions, and over all the power of the enemy, and nothing will injure you. Nevertheless* **do not** *rejoice in this, that the spirits are subject to you, but rejoice that your names are recorded in*

Heaven" (Luke 10:18-20). Jesus said, "Don't rejoice in this." Why? "Because I saw satan fall from Heaven."

The way I read it, and I may be wrong, but the way I read it is that Jesus was saying, "Listen. Don't allow pride to come in, because the very thing that is beginning to work in your life right now, that sense of power, authority, and *superiority* is the very thing that caused satan to be thrown out of Heaven. I was there. I saw it happen. So don't rejoice in this—simply rejoice that your name is written in the Lamb's book of life."

We can never take the glory. We can never take the credit for what we've accomplished because it's only by the grace of God that we can do anything. It's all because of what He does through us. In and of ourselves we have absolutely nothing to boast about.

Remember: It's Not About You

A friend of mine tells the story of the farmyard animals, who at the end of the day are reporting in about their day's activities. All the animals gather together in the barn, and the rooster begins. "I was up before everybody else, announcing the new day." Then the cow gives her report about how she "faithfully supplied the farmer with milk." One by one they share about the day's events.

Meanwhile the donkey is patiently waiting, pacing back and forth. Finally it's his turn and he exclaims, "You won't believe my day. This was the greatest day in my life! I wish you'd have been there to see me. I still can't get over what happened." Everyone was listening in amazement as he shared. "Today I walked down the main road of Jerusalem. Thousands upon thousands of people were there lining the road. They had their palm branches and were waving them at me and crying out, 'Hosanna, hosanna.' Oh,

I mean, it was incredible! I felt so loved, so adored, and so important. I'll never forget this day as long as I live."

My friend concludes the story by saying, "The problem is, the donkey forgot about who was riding on his back."

Sometimes we're like that with our ministry, aren't we? We begin to think that it's all about us and what we've done. We forget that it's the anointing of the Spirit of God resting upon us—and without that we could do absolutely nothing. We take the glory so readily, don't we? We begin to feel that we are just a little better than everybody else. God hates that sort of thing. It's nothing less than rotten old pride.

Nebuchadnezzar was strutting around the roof of his palace one day, admiring all that he had built and accomplished. *"Is this not Babylon the great, which I myself have built...by the might of my power and for the glory of my majesty"* (Dan. 4:30). God immediately spoke to Nebuchadnezzar, informing him that his sovereignty has been taken from him and that he is to find his place among the beasts of the field until he recognizes that God alone had given him the ability to do all he had done.

Likewise, if we are going to survive the anointing we need to continually recognize that we cannot take any credit for our accomplishments. Rather we need to give the glory to the One to whom it is due.

It is so easy, especially in ministry, after a period of time, to feel that you're just a little more relevant or important than others. These days, of course, we have the whole resurgence of emphasis on the fivefold ministry: the apostle, prophet, evangelist, pastor, and teacher. And although I believe that God is restoring the Church's understanding of the important and vital role each is to play, I almost hate to see it—because everybody now wants the recognition and the sense of entitlement that they believe goes with it.

Over the course of the last few years we've seen a growing emphasis on the fivefold ministry. It began with the recognition of the prophetic office; and seemingly overnight we spawned a zillion new "prophets." Since then we have seen the emergence of the apostolic office gain in strength and popularity.

I have in my possession two e-mails that I received within a few days of each other. The first was a serious call to pray for America prior to the invasion of Iraq. The letter urged the Church to fast and pray over a 40-day period. It was signed by a woman who called herself "National Apostle." My concern is that I've seen this woman go from a humble intercessor, to a general of intercessors, then to a prophetic role, and now finally to that of "national apostle." What's next..."Pope"? I for one would love to see a little sprinkling of humility in some of these super-saints. After all, didn't Jesus say that *"and whoever wishes to be first among you shall be slave of all"* (Mark 10:44)?

Although the first e-mail grieved my spirit, the second one gave me hope that all is not lost. Allow me to share the first part of it with you:

> *I'm just a little preacher in the dirt. I'm just a servant in the dirt. I just sit with people in the dirt, with the poor, nothing special. I believe revival has a face. The Lord has given me a life message. He said, "Heidi, revival has a face," and He gave me the story of the good Samaritan. He says, "Revival has a face. You have to see the face. You have to see the face," and so He took me to a nation where I knew nothing. I didn't know the language; I didn't know anything. He sat me with the poor. In fact, I've been sitting with the poor for 20 years.*

What a contrast there is between these two e-mails! Both of these women are very well-known. One is in Mozambique, and I can mention her name because she's humble, so she gets my recognition. *"Humble yourself and you'll be exalted"* (see James 4:10). So let me exalt her. Heidi Baker is an incredible woman of God. If you've ever heard her, she just moves you to tears. I had the joy of ministering with her in Idaho. The meetings were held in a barn, a literal barn, at the county fairgrounds. The cattle shed had no air conditioning, and it was about 95 degrees. There was straw on the ground, and people brought their own chairs to sit on. At either end of the barn were two huge doors that were left open to allow in some fresh air. All during the meetings pigeons were flying in and roosting overhead. It was literally the crudest place I've ever ministered in America, and yet that was one of the greatest conferences I've ever attended.

Heidi had flown all the way from Mozambique just to speak for two days then fly back. I was immediately impressed with her humility as she would just sit down in the straw and lift her face to God as she cried out for His help. She and her husband Roland have been used by the Lord to raise up several thousand churches across Mozambique. They have seen some of the most amazing miracles, and some of the stories she tells are almost beyond belief.

But notice the way she begins her e-mail, "I'm just a *little* preacher sitting in dirt." No wonder God is able to entrust her with so much authority.

I'm greatly concerned about this whole area of men and women who love to parade their "callings." Like the Pharisees of old, they love to be called "Apostle," "Prophet," etc. Whatever happened to "SERVANT"?

Let's always remember the words of the greatest of them all when He said, *"Learn of Me; for I am meek and lowly"* (Matt. 11:29 KJV).

Consider the following account from George Whitefield, considered by many as the greatest preacher of the 18th century. Even to this day his messages are prized by tens of thousands of preachers around the world.

The Churches Are Too Small

On Wednesday evening, Bow Church in Cheapside was exceedingly crowded. I preached my sermon on "Early Piety" and at the request of the societies, printed it. For the next three successive months, there was no end of people flocking to hear the Word of God...Thousands went away from the largest churches for lack of room. They gave their full attention, listening like people concerned for eternity.

I now preached nine times a week. The early communions were awesome. On Sunday morning long before day, you might see streets filled with people going to church. With lanterns in their hands, they conversed about the things of God.... I always preached without a fee.

*The tide of popularity began to run very high. I could no longer walk on foot as usual, but had to go in a coach from place to place to avoid the loud hosannas of the multitude. They grew quite extravagant in their applause. Had it not been for my compassionate Jesus, **popularity would have destroyed me**. I used to plead with Him to take me by the hand and lead my unhurt through this fiery furnace. He heard my request and allowed me to see the vanity of all applause except His own.[2]*

Who today would refer to this type of success as a "firey furnace"? Most of us would relish this type of applause never perceiving its subtle and insidious poison of pride. The Psalmist said it so well when he penned the words, *"Not to us, O Lord, not to us, but to Thy name give glory."*

In closing this chapter let me pass on to you a letter sent by Madame Guyon to an unknown recipient.

Letters of Madame Guyon

HUMILITY THE EFFECT OF LOVE

I assure you, you are very dear to me. I rejoice very much in the progress of your soul. When I speak of progress, it is in descending, not in mounting. As when we charge a vessel, the more ballast we put in, the lower it sinks, so the more love we have in the soul, the lower we are abased in self. The side of the scales which is elevated, is empty; so the soul is elevated only when it is void of love. "Love is our weight," says St. Augustine. Let us so charge ourselves with the weight of love, as to bring down self to its just level. Let its depths be manifested by our readiness to bear the cross, the humiliation, the sufferings, which are necessary to the purification of the soul. Our humiliation is our exaltation. "Whosoever is least among you shall be the greatest," says our Lord.

*I love you, my dear child, in the love of the Divine Master, who so abased Himself by love! Oh! What a weight is love, since it caused so astonishing a fall from Heaven to earth—from God to man! There is a beautiful passage in the **Imitation of Christ**, "Love to be unknown." Let us die to all but God.[3]*

To survive the anointing, we must have humility.

Endnotes

1. Jeanne Guyon, *Spiritual Writings of Madame Guyon* (Seedsowers, 1982), 258.

2. John Wesley, *The Nature of Revival* (Bethany House Publishers, 1987), 68.

3. Madame Guyon, *Spiritual Writings* (Goleta, CA: Christian Books, 1982), 22.

Chapter 8

Worship

God saves men to make them worshipers. Fascination is another element in true worship. To be filled with moral excitement. To be captivated and charmed and entranced. Excited, not with how big you're getting or how big the offering was. Not with how many people came out to church. But entranced with who God is, and struck with astonished wonder at the inconceivable elevation and magnitude and splendor of Almighty God.

—A.W. Tozer

It is a serious mistake to be so preoccupied with living for God as not to have time for living with God, adoring Him, listening to Him, worshiping Him, and consciously resting in His love.

—Salvation Army; Chosen to Be a Soldier

W E now come to the number one priority of the Christian life: worship. *"Thou shalt worship the Lord thy God"* (Matt. 4:10 KJV). *"Love the Lord your God with all your heart, and with all your soul, and with all your mind, and with all your strength"* (Mark 12:30). Worship is one of those rarest of all activities in the church. We really know so little about it. Around ten years ago now, I began to do a little inquiry into what true worship entailed.

We have grown accustomed to using "praise" and "worship" interchangeably. We toss around these terms—"We've got a new worship leader tonight. Let's welcome him; give him a hand," or "Wasn't that a great time of praise tonight?"—and we just get so used to using those words that way. However, I believe that there's a difference between praise and worship.

My father used to say, "Prayer is preoccupation with our needs; praise is preoccupation with our blessings; and worship is preoccupation with God alone." Prayer is preoccupation with our needs: "God heal me," "God bless me," "God protect me," whatever our needs are, we present them to God. That's prayer.

Praise, then, is preoccupation with our blessings. "Thank You for healing me," "Thank You for blessing me," "Thank You for watching over me," "Thank You..." for whatever it is that God has done for us.

But worship is preoccupation with God, regardless of our circumstances. You may be surprised to learn that the greatest acts of worship, anywhere in the Word of God, were never associated with music. Let me say that again: The greatest acts of worship in the Word of God were never in association with music. Now that doesn't mean you can't worship with music. I'm simply saying that it is not a necessity to have music in order to worship. Worship goes far beyond the musical realm; it deals with my attitude toward God, but also deals with and reveals my heart.

Let me take you to Luke chapter 17, a favorite passage of mine:

Which of you, having a slave plowing or tending sheep, will say to him when he has come in from the field, "Come immediately and sit down to eat"? But will he not say to him, "Prepare something for me to eat, properly clothe yourself and serve me, while I eat and drunk; and afterward you may eat and drink." He does not thank the slave because he did the things which were commanded, does he? So you too, when you do all these things which are commanded you, say, "We are unworthy slaves; we have only done that which we ought to have done" (Luke 17:7-10).

Now notice the picture: Here is a master and his slave. The slave is involved in two aspects of work; he's either plowing or tending sheep. In other words, he's serving his master's interests. There are two major types of ministry: *evangelistic* and *pastoral*. Evangelism involves plowing the fields, going out, knocking on doors, breaking open the fallow ground, and sowing the seed, as well as prayer and intercession. The pastoral side of ministry includes the care of the flock, as well as encouraging, nurturing, teaching, counseling, and caring. And so we have two major aspects of ministry.

We Were Created To Serve the Master

Imagine yourself as the slave, serving your master. You come in at the end of the day, tired and exhausted. You simply want to sit down, kick back, and have something to eat. But then your master calls you, "Before you do anything else, go clean up, properly clothe yourself, and prepare something for me to eat, then you can eat." Now you could have a bit of an attitude, couldn't you, if that was you? After all you've been serving your master out in the freezing rain or blistering heat while he's been sitting inside his comfortable home all day. You could think to yourself, *They're not my sheep; they're his sheep. It's not my field; it's his field.* Most of us would say to ourselves at the end of the day, *Hey, give me a little bit of time to myself.* But notice in this story that the needs of the master come before anything else. This is a true picture of worship. I believe it was Robert Murray McCheyne who said, "No amount of activity in the King's service will make up for the neglect of the King Himself."

Worship is properly preparing ourselves to come into His presence and then bowing before Him in humble adoration for no other reason than God Himself. Yes, we may be involved in leading a home group or a cell group, teaching a Bible study, or be out on the streets witnessing, but our utmost calling and number one priority is God Himself.

Worship is to draw aside and come into the presence of God, properly clothed, washed, prepared, with the desire of satisfying the needs of our Master. There is no higher calling; it's the one eternal calling of the Church. After all the church planning, after all the evangelism is done, all the prophesying, all the signs, wonders, and miracles are finished, a million years from now we will still be lost in worship. It makes sense then that we need to learn about worship, doesn't it?

Before I reached my teens my father began traveling from England to the United States. He would be away from home for weeks if not months at a time. In the early 1950s he was asked to minister for A.W. Tozer, who was pastoring in Chicago at the time. In the middle of the night the fire alarms went off in the hotel where my father was staying. My father opened his door, and found the hallway filled with smoke. There was no way of escape. He closed the door and went to a window—he was on the third or fourth floor. He opened the window and proceeded to jump down. On the way down God gave him a verse, *"You shall not die, but live, and declare the glory of God"* (see Ps. 188:17). Seconds later he hit the ground, smashed up his feet, broke one leg in three places, the other leg in two places, and broke his back in two or three places. After lying there for some time he was taken to the hospital, where he was left unattended in a hallway, his body covered with a sheet. A little while later he heard two of the doctors saying, "Leave him. He's going to die."

My father had just enough strength to pull aside the sheet and say, "Are you talking about me?" He was 44 years of age at the time, and he didn't die till age 87. While in the hospital my father was placed in a full body cast from his chin to his toes. One day he found himself complaining a little, "Lord, You've just begun to open doors for ministry, but now what good am I? I can't preach. I can't even read my Bible." He was sort of having a little bit of a pity party, when he heard the Spirit of God say, "You can learn to worship. You can learn to worship."

Remember that regardless of your circumstances, His "worthship" is still the same. There is an old law of Bible interpretation called "the law of first mention." Many of the old teachers and expositors used to refer to it. It simply means that when a truth is mentioned for the first time in Scripture, it usually conveys vital information as to how that "truth" is to be understood from that time on. The very first time that worship is ever mentioned in the Word of God is in relation to the life of Abraham.

Now at this point, Abraham has already been tested over and over again by the Lord. He has shown to the Lord his willingness to forsake father and mother. He has left behind his relatives, his home, and his country in order to follow the Lord his God. The years have passed and Abraham has become the father of Isaac. The boy is starting to develop and Abraham and Isaac have formed an incredible bond.

One day God looks down, and He sees Abraham and Isaac relating together, and He says, "*Abraham, come here. I want you to* *take your son, your only son **whom thou lovest**, and put him on the altar"* (see Gen. 22:1-2). The Bible tells us in the very next verse that "Abraham rose early in the morning." What a beautiful little statement. Oh, if there was ever a morning to sleep in, that was the morning. If that had been me, the night before I would have pulled the blinds, taken a couple of sleeping tablets, then pulled the blankets over my head attempting to postpone the inevitable.

But no, not Abraham. He jumps out of bed early that morning, saddles his donkey, prepares the wood, takes some of his servants, and commences a three-day journey. After three days of travel God says, "This is the place." Abraham turns to his servants and tells them, "Stay here, I and the lad will go yonder, and we will worship." This is the first mention of worship in the Bible; there is no choir, no instruments, no voices, just radical obedience.

After building the altar and placing Isaac upon it, Abraham raises his knife to slay his son. Suddenly God declares from Heaven, *"Do not stretch out your hand against the lad...for now I know that you fear God, since you have not withheld your son, your only son, from Me"* (Gen. 22:12). Notice something: This time, when referring to Isaac, God did not add "whom thou lovest." The reason being that now the Lord knew that Abraham's love for Him surpassed that of his love for Isaac. You see, whatever you *withhold* is what you *worship*. Whatever God cannot have in your life, has more importance to you than God Himself. *"Because you have not withheld, therefore I will bless you"* (see Gen. 22:16-17). If you want the blessing of God, there can be no withholding. If you withhold your money, you love money more than God. If you withhold some friendship, you love that friendship more than God. Whatever it is that you withhold is ultimately what you worship.

So, you see, worship gets right to the very root of who we are, our relationship with God. Webster defines worship in his 1828 edition dictionary: "to honor with extravagant love and extreme submission." That's his definition. To *worship* is "to honor with extravagant love and extreme submission." Oh I would say that was true of Abraham; it shows extravagant love to give your only son and extreme submission to be willing to pick up a knife and kill the joy of your life.

Examples From the Bible of Worshipers

I've looked into the Word for the best examples of worship. I love the heart of David, whom we all regard as the great worshiper of the Old Testament. I have come to believe that David's greatest act of worship occurred after he committed adultery with Bathsheba and became the father of her child (see 2 Sam. 12:15-25). Shortly after the birth of their son, the baby was stricken with a fever and David withdrew to pray for the child. For seven days, he appeared to be wrestling with God in prayer to spare the life of his son. On the seventh day, the child died. I can imagine how David could have been angry toward God. He could have said, "Listen, I thought we had settled the score." It's recorded in Psalm 51:4,7 that David said, "*Against Thee, Thee only, have I sinned.... Purge me with hyssop, and I shall be clean: wash me, and I shall be whiter than snow.*"

David could have said, "Lord, I thought we'd dealt with this. You know, after all, this baby didn't sin. I sinned, and I thought You had forgiven me." He could have had a theological debate; he could have had a temper tantrum spiritually—but he didn't. The Bible says that he got off his face, went into his room, washed himself, prepared himself, went right back into the presence of God, and got down and worshiped. There was no music—just total surrender before God. The Bible clearly states, "*As for God, 'His work is perfect'*" (Deut. 32:4), and "The clay can never say to the Potter, why?"

David is not there to question God; he's just simply there to bow and say, "Lord, You're right in all of Your ways. You're perfect in all of Your ways." What a beautiful picture of worship. Yes, it was costly. Yes, David was hurting. But David knew that despite his circumstances, God's "worth-ship" was still the same.

I've come to believe that the greatest act of worship is found in the story of Job. You know the story, how the devil paid God a visit one day. I think it sort of went like this. As the devil was about to leave, God said, "Oh, by the way, before you go, devil, see that man over there? Do you recognize him?"

The devil says, "Should I?"

God replies, "Yes."

"But I don't recognize him," says the devil.

"I didn't think so; that's Job."

"You're kidding. Job?"

"Yes. I picked him up off your trash heap when he was riddled with AIDS and about to die."

You see, we're introduced to Job in the Bible as a God-fearing, honest, upright man, who turned away from evil and so on, but nobody is born that way. The Bible says, *"there is none righteous, no, not one"* (Rom. 3:10 NKJV). So what we see in Job is a product of God's grace, so I believe the scenario went something like this. God picked him up one day, riddled with sin, maybe a wife-beater, maybe an alcoholic, perhaps having one of the foulest mouths in the region. But then God in His grace comes along and lifts *"the beggar from the dunghill and makes him a prince with God"* (see 1 Sam. 2:8 KJV). God loves to brag about His workmanship, doesn't He?

We have a beautiful picture of this following the creation of each day, in that we see God admiring His handiwork, declaring, "It is good" (see Gen. 1). We are somewhat similar, in that when we make something, we like to take a little bit of credit for it, don't we? The Bible says, *"We are His workmanship"* (Eph. 2:10). I think God was just reminding everyone of who really deserves the credit, and He said, "Satan, see what I made out of that trash of yours?"

I think the devil said, "You know, I don't believe that's Job."

He said, "Yes, it is."

The devil said, "OK, but when I corrupt, I absolutely corrupt, and Your grace is not sufficient to change what I corrupt."

God says, "Yes, it is."

Satan says, "No, it's not. The only reason this man is acting the way he is, is because You've made him a multimillionaire. You've given him thousands of cattle; You've blessed him financially; no wonder he acts so pious."

Finally God turns to the devil and says, "Listen, he's genuine, right to the very core. In fact," He said, "I'll let you place him under any test, and I'll show you how genuine he really is. There is only one rule: You can't take his life."

To this challenge, the devil says, "OK, You're on."

The following day Job buries ten children—seven sons, three daughters, ten caskets there at the local graveyard. Can you imagine having a test like that to go through? Some of you may have lost the life of a child, but ten children? All in the same day? It appears from the Scriptures that they were married, that they had their own homes. It is possible that standing there with Job and his wife are the remaining spouses and perhaps their children.

The next picture is that of Job covered in boils from the top of his head to the soles of his feet. Great sores running with puss that drive him almost crazy with pain and no amount of scratching seems to give him any relief. Here is this great man reduced to nothing, both physically and financially. We see him sitting in the ashes. I personally believe that perhaps this was all that remained of his once magnificent mansion. Now there is nothing left, just a mound of ashes. We see Job trying to rummage through to find something to relieve the pain, and all he can find is a broken piece of his wife's favorite dinnerware set, maybe an anniversary gift. Everything is in smithereens, and he pulls this shard out of the ashes and begins to scratch himself, trying to get some sort of relief. His wife says, "Why don't you just finish it? Curse God and die. Let God judge you. Curse Him and He'll strike you dead, and then it will be all over. You'll be out of your pain, out of your misery."

But instead, the Bible says, *"Job got on his face and he worshiped"* (see Job 1:20). No choir, no stringed instruments, no music, just a man bowing in absolute surrender before God and no doubt thinking in his heart, *"As for God, His work is perfect"* (see Deut. 32:4).

Modern-Day Worshipers

You see worship reveals the heart, doesn't it? Worship reveals whether we really know and honor God or not. God is looking for worshipers, which is why that should be our number one priority.

I mentioned earlier that my father was caught in a blazing hotel fire and was forced to jump out of the window in order to save his life. One of the blessings that resulted from that experience was that my father developed a close bond with A.W. Tozer. Tozer said to my dad, "Len, if you're ever in Chicago, just stop by my office anytime. You've got an open invitation. Stop by, and we'll let our hair down," was his expression. In other words, "Let's be real with each other."

My father tells how one afternoon around 2:00 or 3:00 p.m., he went to Tozer's office. During the course of the conversation, Tozer said to him, "You know, Len, I had so much to do this morning. I came into the office here, and I got down on this little rug...." It was just a little threadbare rug, as my father describes it. Tozer went on. "When you knocked on the door," he said, "I just got off my knees to answer the door. I haven't even started to pray yet, all I've done is worship."

You wonder why Tozer wrote the way he wrote? Tozer was the sort of man who could just get lost in the presence of God, the majesty of God, just carried away. *"When I consider the heavens, the work of Your hands, the sun, and the moon, and the stars which You have made, what is man?"* (see Ps. 8:3-4). All of a sudden he would just find himself lost in God's greatness and majesty and the hours would slip by without his being aware of it. That's worship.

I recall hearing Jack Hayford describing those living beings in Revelation who just consistently bow down and cry "Holy, Holy, Holy." Hayford said, "You know, they're not on some sort of mechanical timer or anything like that. But rather," he said, "they lift up their eyes, and they see God as they've never seen Him before—like when a diamond catches the light and all the various hues shine forth. Every time these beings gaze upon the Lord they marvel at the immensity of God and therefore continually bow down before Him crying, 'Holy, Holy, Holy.'" It's something we'll spend eternity doing, so why not begin to practice now?

It's almost impossible to lose the anointing and still remain a worshiper. However, the reverse is also true: If you remain a worshiper, it will be impossible to lose the anointing.

Chapter 9

Diversity/Variety

For each one of us there is a special vocation in which we can follow Christ. I do not believe that all of you would be following him if you were to attempt to preach. Even Christ never attempted to do what His Father did not intend Him to do. A man once asked Him to officiate as a lawyer or judge, but He replied, "Who made Me a judge or a divider over you?" One beauty of Christ's life was that He kept to His calling and did not go beyond His commission. And you will be wise if you do the same.

—Charles H. Spurgeon

I now want us to consider the matter of *diversity or variety.* Another safeguard to surviving the anointing has to do with understanding the importance of diversity. God is a God of infinite variety and diversity. Consider the billions of tons of snow that fall in a single season and then just ponder the fact that no two snowflakes are the same. Each one has a unique pattern all their own—how much more His own people?

Someone once defined "burnout" as the thing that happens when you try to walk in another person's calling or anointing. Each of us has our own unique calling and purpose. The Body of Christ, like our natural body, consists of many members. Each member has its part to play if the body is going to function naturally. As I mentioned earlier in this book, there are some 1,500 ministers a month dropping out of the ministry, primarily due to moral failure, but the second reason is "burnout."

Why is it that we are always looking at somebody else's methods or style and then we try to emulate what they are doing? If God has not called us to do something, we will soon find out that we are "kicking against the pricks." In other words, we are going contrary to what the Lord has called us to do.

God has given me the calling of a teacher to the Body of Christ. If I were to step into the realm of an evangelist, I would soon grow frustrated and become exhausted trying to fill somebody else's shoes. Most evangelists are more dramatic and outgoing than I am. To make an attempt to copy their style would go in violation of my nature and calling. The end result being burnout.

We need to understand that God is a God of diversity. All we have to do is look around us. We all have two ears, two eyes, a nose, and a mouth, and yet we are all so different.

In Paul's letter to the Corinthians, he explains to the church that there is a variety of gifts, but the same Spirit; varieties of ministry, but the same Lord. There are varieties of effects, but the same God who works all things in all persons. Notice again, variety of gifts, variety of ministries, variety of effects, yet we are a body, and our body is unique. It has a variety of members, and all those members have a different function, yet they're all vital. They're all essential; you can't do without one. *"If the hand should say to the foot, 'I have no need of thee,' or the eye should say to the hand, 'I have no need of thee...,'"* Paul says (see 1 Cor. 12). We need to recognize the diversity that God has placed in the Body of Christ.

In Ephesians we read that God has given to the Church: apostles, prophets, evangelists, pastors, and teachers. Each office has its own function to perform in bringing the Church to the fullness of Christ. I was taught that:

The Apostle.......Governs.

The Prophet.......Guides.

The Evangelist....Gathers.

The Pastor.........Guards.

The Teacher......Grounds.

The apostolic gift is primarily governmental. Paul stated that he was a wise master builder. He understood the need for proper structure and government within the Church. The prophet is often used by the Lord to confirm and encourage as well as to warn the Church regarding the direction they are going. The evangelist has an anointing to gather as well as inspire the Church to reach out to others. The pastor is the shepherd who carefully and compassionately watches over the well-being of God's flock. The teacher is called to ground the Church in the Word of God, to lay a foundation of doctrinal beliefs that will keep them firmly rooted in Christ.

The Body of Christ Needs Teamwork

I'm convinced that one of the greatest tragedies in the church world today is the lack of "team ministry." We have too many men trying to "go it alone." As a result they become frustrated and the Church lacks the balance and blessing that can only be achieved through God-ordained "leaders." We readily accept the fact that children are better off having two parents. The father plays a role in his child's development that his wife can't fill, and likewise the wife plays a role that her husband can't fill. Why is it then that when it comes to the family of God we think the pastor can provide everything the "family" needs?

I love observing the diversity of God as revealed through His many servants. Over the course of my life, I have had the privilege of working with some of God's choicest servants. My wife and I commenced our ministry in New York City in the mid-1960s working with David Wilkerson (founder of Teen Challenge). We later joined Loren Cunningham in the early days of Youth With A Mission (YWAM). Some leaders we have had the privilege to know are household names, while others will not be known until eternity. Each of them has or had their own unique "flavor."

For example, on several occasions I sat under the ministry of John Wimber, as well as another man of God, Mahesh Chavda. Both of those men have (or had) very outstanding healing ministries. Mahesh is still alive, whereas John has gone to be with the Lord. They both taught on healing and how the Lord had led them to pray for the sick. John Wimber used to emphasize over and over that when you pray for somebody you should never close your eyes, but rather *look at the person.* John had all sorts of reasons why it was important to keep your eyes open while praying. To tell you the truth (confession time), I could never really grasp what he meant.

I later had the opportunity to listen to Mahesh share some of the insights the Lord had taught him through the course of his ministry. Mahesh has seen some amazing healings, especially in Africa. One of the greatest revelations he received was from reading the account of Lazarus' being raised from the dead. Mahesh related that when Jesus came to the tomb He raised His eyes to the Father and then commanded Lazarus to come forth. He shared how the Lord had quickened to him *not to look at the problem but to look to the Lord.*

I chuckled to myself and thought, *God cannot be reduced down to some formula.* There are varieties of workings but the same Spirit. Here are two great men of God, one is saying, "Keep your eyes open and [basically] look at the problem," and the other revelation was, "Whatever you do, don't look at the problem; look to the Lord."

I've also had the occasion to be in several of Kathryn Kuhlman's meetings and have watched as the Spirit of God settled like a cloud over the meeting. Kuhlman would simply call out what she was receiving from the Lord as she pointed to people all over the auditorium whom the Lord was touching. I don't recall her ever bringing people forward to be prayed for, but rather they came forward to testify of what the Lord had already done during the meeting.

On the other hand, we have all seen men and women of God call people forward and pray for them one by one in some type of healing line. I'm convinced that God works through all these methods to keep us dependent upon Him rather than on some so-called proven method that we might come to rely upon.

Who Is Jesus to You?

Matthew chapter 16 records the well-known incident of when Jesus asked Peter, *"Who do you say that I am?"* This question was preceded by Jesus first asking His disciples, *"Who do people say that the Son of Man is?"* Their response is, *"Some say John the Baptist; and others, Elijah; but still others, Jeremiah, or one of the prophets"* (Matt. 16:14).

I began to ponder this one day as to how people came to such varied opinions of who Jesus was. Some say Elijah; some say John the Baptist; some say Jeremiah. Those three characters could not be more diverse. The Bible says of John the Baptist, *"John did no miracles"* (see John 10:41). John didn't perform any miracles, according to the Word of God. Now how could you possibly go with Jesus for a couple of days and end up saying, "He's just like John the Baptist"? The Scriptures tell us that Jesus went about doing good and healing all who were oppressed of the devil, yet we have evidence of no such thing happening through John the Baptist's ministry.

Perhaps somebody followed Jesus one day and saw Him stand in front of the Pharisees and tell them, "Listen, you bunch of whitewashed tombs, outwardly you appear to be immaculate, but inside, you're like an open sewer" (see Matt. 23:27). That's not exactly a "seeker-sensitive" way to open a pastor's conference.

On another occasion Jesus said to the same Pharisees and Scribes, "Prostitutes and tax gathers will get into the kingdom of God before you."

Now if you heard Jesus speaking that way, you'd think, "Wow, He's just like John the Baptist—black and white, in your face, forthright, no mincing of words. He says it like it is. He's just like John."

Then somebody else says, "No, no, no, I don't know where you get this John the Baptist stuff. I've been with Him for three days now, and He's just like Elijah. You should have seen the demons He cast out, not to mention the numerous healings plus all types of miracles. I saw Him feeding the 5,000, raising the dead. I mean, He's got the power of Elijah."

And then somebody else voices their opinion, "You guys are both wrong. You're crazy. I spent a couple of days with Him. In fact, just yesterday I was with Him, and He was weeping like a baby, weeping over Jerusalem, absolutely broken. I've never seen a man so compassionate, so broken. Shortly after that, there was a group of little street urchins running around, and the disciples were trying to get rid of them, and Jesus said, 'Hey, don't get rid of the children. Bring them to Me.' And I watched Him take those little ones and put them on His lap, and cradle them in His arms. He was just like a loving grandfather. He's just like Jeremiah, the weeping prophet. His compassion, His mercy, His tenderness are without question."

We Need Elijahs, John the Baptists, and Jeremiahs

You see, all three of those characteristics were true of the Lord Jesus Christ. He was the voice of "many waters." But the day came when that corn of wheat had to fall into the ground and die, otherwise it would abide alone. You see, the earthly body of Jesus Christ could only be in one place at one time. If He was in Bethany, He couldn't be in Nazareth. If He was in Nazareth, He couldn't be in Jericho. And if He was in Jericho, He couldn't be in Jerusalem, and so on.

But that corn of wheat fell into the ground, and as a result it brought forth much fruit. And as a result of that fruit, we now have the John the Baptists, and we have the Jeremiahs, and we have the Elijahs, and so on, because we have now the mystical Body of Christ, if I could put it that way. This mystical Body contains everything that you see in the life of the Lord Jesus Christ. Some people are called to thunder forth like John the Baptist; others will have that tenderness that causes them to break and weep; while still others will be raised up by God to perform healings and miracles.

So there is great diversity in the Body, and we need to understand that uniqueness; otherwise we can become cynical and judgmental of others whose ministries may differ from our own. It is therefore important to remain in the calling to which you were called. Don't try to be something you're not; otherwise you're going to frustrate yourself and simply burn out.

There is a wonderful sense of rest and peace when we operate in our God-given calling. God wants to free us within the framework of our own personality. That doesn't mean that when you're "free," you automatically become sanguine, or an extrovert. It means that you are free within the personality that God has given you.

Find your God-given calling and anointing and stay there—you'll survive.

Chapter 10

Family

It was a great joy to me when my sons were born, but it was an infinitely surpassing joy as they told me they had sought and found the Savior. To pray with them, to point them yet more fully to Christ, to hear the story of their spiritual troubles, and to help them out of their spiritual difficulties was an intense satisfaction to my soul.

—Charles H. Spurgeon

ALTHOUGH the family may not be directly tied to surviving the anointing, I do believe that there is a vital link. Leaders need to make sure that they do not neglect their families. I don't recall ever speaking to a man of God in leadership who, if he had to live his life all over again, would not spend more time with his family. It is so easy to get caught up in the demands of ministry and neglect your own family.

Don't Steal in Order to Give

Sometime back in the mid-1970s our church invited Ern Baxter to be our guest speaker at our annual Christmas church conference. During one of his messages he made the following statement, "God is not interested in stolen time." He then proceeded to share about when, as a young minister, he was in his office preparing a message. One or two of his children came asking him to play with them; and rather harshly, he told them he was too busy and asked them to leave him alone. No sooner had the children left when he heard the Lord speaking; "Ern, I'm not interested in stolen time." In other words, God was saying, "You are taking time that rightfully belongs to your children, and you are giving it to Me under the guise of ministry." I remember thinking about my own children and how the demands of the church had gradually caused me to sacrifice them on the altar of ministry. I had become too busy looking after everybody else's vineyard, so to speak, but not taking care of my own.

With Ern's statement still ringing in my ears, I needed to find some scriptural support for it. I said to the Lord, "I want to see that principle in the Word of God." It bore witness in my spirit, but I said, "Where is it in the Word?" The very next day I happened to turn to Matthew 15:1-2 (NKJV), where it tells about some Pharisees and Scribes who came to Jesus from Jerusalem with a question, "Why do Your disciples transgress the tradition of the elders? For they do not wash their hands when they eat bread?"

Here was a delegation who came to Jesus with a question regarding one of their traditions. They had become alarmed at the fact that Jesus of all people was permitting His disciples to eat without washing their hands. Jesus, not being deterred for a moment, asked them why they violated the commands of God. Traditions are simply that, *traditions*. But commands are far more serious business. One relates to culture, the other to God Himself. Jesus explains, *"For God says, 'Honor your father and mother; he that speaks evil of father or mother, let him be put to death.' But you say, 'Whoever shall say to his father or mother, "anything of mine that you might have been helped by is being given to God." He is not to honor his father and his mother,' and thus you invalidate the Word of God for the sake of your traditions"* (see Matt. 15:4-6).

In other words, what was happening here was that they were taking money that rightfully belonged to their parents. After all, there was no social security in those days, and it was the responsibility of children as they got older to provide for their aged parents who could no longer work to support themselves. These so-called spiritual leaders were putting the needs of the synagogue or the temple before the needs of their own flesh and blood. Consequently they were breaking the commandment of God. They used the term "Corbin" or sacrifice to God to excuse themselves from helping their parents. Jesus exposed their hypocrisy and in essence was saying, "God is not interested in stolen money."

I had found the principle I was looking for. There are certain things that God is not interested in: stolen things. Anytime we offer to God something that we have wrongfully taken from another, God will have no part in it. This is especially true when it comes to the family. I can so easily neglect my wife and family under the guise of ministry. Hebrews tells us how Noah prepared an ark for the salvation of his house. The reason that Noah built an ark was not simply to put all the animals in it. No, the main reason he was building an ark was for the salvation of his household. Why? Because God was going to bring judgment. The world was corrupt, utterly corrupt. God saw the thoughts of men that their hearts were "only evil continually," and He said, "I'm going to destroy the earth." Noah found grace in the eyes of the Lord, and he prepared an ark for the *salvation* of his house.

Godly Fathers Care for Their Families

We are told that *"as it was in the days of Noah, so shall it be at the coming of the Son of man"* (see Luke 17:26-27). We have the responsibility as spiritual Noahs to prepare an ark for the salvation of our households. In other words, we are responsible for our children, our family; we're responsible to provide an atmosphere, a "spiritual ark," where by the grace of God they will be saved. And that will take us almost as much time and effort as it did Noah.

I've always been challenged by Job. We are told that he rose up early every morning to offer sacrifices for his family "lest they had sinned." It would appear from the context that his family was grown and living on their own. Yet here is Job still carrying out his priestly role as the head of his home. Would to God we had more fathers who would take seriously their "headship." Seldom does a day go by that I don't bring my wife, three daughters, two son-in-laws, and grandchildren before the Lord in prayer. I still feel that responsibility to pray for them, pray for wisdom, direction, protection, and blessing upon their lives. Like Noah and Job, we need to prepare an "ark" for the salvation of our family.

We are responsible for meeting our children's spiritual needs. Obviously we can't save them—they come to Christ on the basis of need like everybody else—but we can provide a place of safety and protection. This is a day when, as you know, the thoughts of men are only evil continually, and we need to have a safe haven for our children. The home needs to be a place of joy, a place where they like to be, rather than want to leave. As the God-ordained leaders of our home, we need to provide a place of joy, godliness, provision, and protection, so that our family members are not looking to the world to meet their needs. There is no greater indictment against a man of God than to hear that he met the needs of others but failed to meet the needs of his own family.

Chapter 11

Adversary

Those who are to lead in the fight must be prepared to see their comrades fall, as well as the enemy, and must be willing to stand alone, if need be, grasping the standard even in death.

—Frederick Booth-Tucker,
Life of Catherine Booth, Vol. 1

In war, none are permitted to err twice.

—John Trapp

ANYONE who has spent any time at all in the ministry will soon realize that they are up against the enemy. In his wonderful book, *Discipler's Manual*, F.E. Marsh states, "There are three enemies that oppose the Christian. These are *internal*, *external*, and *infernal*." The first, *the internal enemy*, is the evil principle that is called the "flesh." The second, *the external enemy*, is the "world." The third, *the infernal enemy*, is satan, along with all the hosts of evil under him.

Ministry and spiritual warfare go hand in hand. Peter was well aware of this when he said, *"Your adversary the devil goes around as a roaring lion seeking whom he may devour"* (see 1 Pet. 5:8). We have an adversary. We need to understand that. It is absolutely imperative if you and I are going to survive the anointing. The enemy is out to do everything that he is capable of doing to undermine and sabotage what God is doing in and through your life. And it's only as we become aware of this strategy that we will survive.

Recognize the Enemy

Paul says, *"We are not ignorant concerning his devices"* (2 Cor. 2:11). We have to recognize that the enemy comes in different ways; he masquerades in different forms. Sometimes he comes as a roaring lion. If a roaring lion came into your room right now, you would be smart enough to get out of his way, imminently aware of the danger you are facing. But the Bible also says that he comes as a wolf in sheep's clothing.

Now I was raised on a farm in Ireland where we had sheep. Then I spent 15 years in New Zealand, where there are around 4 million people and 50-70 million sheep. With that many sheep around, you soon begin to know what they look like. But if you are not familiar with what sheep are like, you might find yourself confronted by a woolly, innocent-looking thing that comes right up to you, then before you have time to react it opens its mouth and you're history—because this was not a sheep at all. It was a wolf in sheep's clothing.

The third, and by far the most deceptive, form the enemy takes is to appear as an angel of light. John Kilpatrick, the former senior pastor of the Assembly of God church in Pensacola, Florida, told the story one Sunday morning about the time when he was a young boy. If I recall correctly, he was all alone at home when he heard somebody walking down the hallway in his home. Suddenly the door of his bedroom opened, and in walked this most beautiful and magnificent being. His immediate reaction was to fall down and worship as he was convinced he was seeing the Lord. Just then something told him to look at the being's hands. John said, "When I looked at his hands, there were no nail prints."

I remember that as he shared that experience, chills went up and down my spine. This was none other than the devil masquerading as an angel of light. It's little wonder that we are warned in God's Word not to be ignorant concerning his devices. All of us would immediately run for cover if he just came in a red suit with horns, a pitchfork, and a long tail. But when he comes appearing to be the Lord Jesus Christ, radiant, glorious, and beautiful, then it may be a little harder to discern. F.E. Marsh says, "Satan comes as a roaring lion to persecute: or as an angel of light to patronize. Satan as an 'angel of light' is far more to be dreaded than satan as 'a roaring lion.' A patronizing enemy is far worse than a persecuting one."

Learn From the Parable of the Sower

In the parable of the sower, we are given some real insights into the area of spiritual warfare and the operation of the enemy. Jesus spoke about four types of ground/soil into which the seed is sown. The seed, according to Matthew's account, is the seed of the Kingdom. The sower is Jesus our King, who is seeking to establish His Kingdom principles within our hearts and lives. Jesus explained that as the seed was sown, some seed fell upon stony ground and was immediately devoured by the birds of the air. Later He explained that this represented the devil. To me this is a picture of the enemy as a "roaring lion." He is easy to see and recognize.

But then Jesus told about those who received the Word and immediately seemed to grow and spring up. All of us enjoy seeing people respond to the Word and then seemingly to make great strides in their Christian walk. The enemy, however, is not finished with his cunning. Not being able to devour the seed, he causes persecution to increase so that after a period of time the seed withers and dies. The process may be somewhat slower, but the end result is the same: God's Word is rendered null and void. I see this as a type of the enemy's coming as a wolf in sheep's clothing. He is more cunning because he uses others to fulfill his diabolical plans.

The third group represents the enemy at "his best." Jesus told of those who receive the Word and begin to grow. They even attempt to bring forth fruit. Now notice something: They have survived the birds of the air. They have withstood the same heat of the sun, or the "persecution" as Jesus called it, but now they are being deceived into thinking that as long as they have received the Word and have some evidence of growth, that's all that really matters. Jesus saw it differently, however. He says that these are the ones who, because of the thorns and thistles, bring no fruit to maturity.

The only reason a person sows seed is to reap a harvest. No farmer in his right mind spends days, if not weeks, preparing the land and then sows the seed only to reap the exact amount he started with. The enemy here comes as the angel of light. These people are not even aware that they are being targeted. How does satan thwart God's purpose? By simply entangling God's people with the riches, worries, and cares of this life. In other words, these people become so busy with the daily activities of living that they no longer have time to serve God. I'm convinced that the enemy can have you promoted so that you no longer have time to serve the Kingdom—because you now have added responsibilities at the office. The enemy cares little whether you attend church or not as long as he can keep you from advancing God's work.

Don't Let the Enemy Weigh You Down

I prided myself for a long time into thinking the devil hadn't take the seed out of my life. I haven't really had to survive any real persecution, as such, but the most subtle attack of the enemy comes through riches, worries, and cares of this life. In Hebrews 11, we are exhorted to lay aside every weight and to run the race. Those of you who are runners know that the less encumbered you are, the more distance you can cover in the least amount of time. The enemy seeks to encumber us with what may appear to be a *blessing* but ends up being a *burden*.

Running was one of the favorite sports 2,000 years ago. Every province had their heroes, similar to today's athletic superstars. There was fierce rivalry between these competing provinces as well as between countries. So great was the pressure to win that every strategy possible was used to gain the advantage and there-fore win. Historical records indicate that one of the favorite strategies was that of placing young women along the route of the runners. These beautiful women would make themselves available to the runners in hope of delaying any athlete who drew aside to satisfy their "youthful lusts." Another ploy used was to roll in front of the runner a ball of solid gold. These "weights" could be the equivalent of a year's salary, if not far more. Sometimes this temptation succeeded in causing the runner to stoop down and pick up the "weight," thinking that he could still run at the same pace. Gradually, however, this weight would sap the runner's energy, giving his opponent the advantage and causing the other to lose.

All one has to do is study the lives of some of God's people to see the devastating results of riches. Although I believe that the Lord does bless His servants, I can also see how many have allowed their blessings to become a burden that ultimately keeps them from moving on with God. It was God Himself who blessed His people Israel with a "land that flowed with milk and honey" but then warned them that it could also cause them to forget Him.

The enemy knows how to slow us down, to get us diverted with this thing or that thing. If it's not sexual temptation, it's financial. Or he causes us to become infatuated with our own position and importance. The enemy will use various strategies and devices to seek to deter us from running and finishing the race.

As an example, take a look at the story of Nehemiah. As soon as Nehemiah began to rebuild the walls of Jerusalem, Sanballat and Tobiah appear on the scene. These men do everything they can to frustrate and discourage those who are building the wall. There will always be a Sanballat and a Tobiah in our life as long as we are seeking to do the work of God.

In order to survive the anointing we need to be aware of the enemy's devices. By ourselves, we are no match for his cunning. It is only as we become strong in the Lord and the strength of His might that we will be able to stand.

This is by no means a detailed study on spiritual warfare, but I trust that it will serve to remind you that we have an enemy and also to remind you that *"greater is He that is in you than he that is in the world"* (1 John 4:4).

Chapter 12

Integrity

Integrity: the entire unimpaired state of anything, particularly of the mind; moral soundness or purity; incorruptness; uprightness; honesty…

—Noah Webster,
1828 edition American Dictionary

Avoid the Appearance of Evil

PARIS, the "city of lights," is known as the most romantic city in the world. Paris is also known for its famous restaurants and scrumptious cuisine—not to mention such famed sights as the Eiffel Tower, the Louvre, or the Avenues de Champs-Elysees, and its ever-popular sidewalk cafés. This was my first time to visit this great city, and I was there, not as a tourist, but rather to minister. Throughout my lifetime, I've traveled extensively around the world and yet have missed many of the famous tourist sights due to busy schedules and time restraints. I was hoping that perhaps this time I would be able to take a few hours and "see the sights."

While there I met a woman whom my wife and I had met several times over the years. Her parents were close friends and spiritual pillars in the church where I served in Christchurch, New Zealand. Susan (not her real name) had been sent out by the church to work and minister in France and was based out of Paris. Although we were not close, we had many mutual friends "back home." Susan attended the conference where I was speaking and asked me if I had had an opportunity to see Paris. I told her that I had gone out one day and had seen the Eiffel Tower. She insisted that the best way to see Paris was by night and offered to drive me around as she had her own car.

First she suggested that she would like to take me to a typical Parisian restaurant where I could enjoy some real French cooking, then we could drive around the city. What a great opportunity to really see this amazing city, plus have my own tour guide! I had absolutely no thought of any impropriety as I gladly accepted her offer.

That afternoon I called home to share with my wife that I had met Susan and that she had offered to take me around Paris. Nancy was not nearly as excited as I was, and I immediately sensed her concern. My initial thought was that she was jealous that I was in Paris and therefore was simply "raining on my parade." The more we talked, however, the more I realized that she was concerned with "the appearance of evil." She then asked me to promise her that I would either not go or else I would have someone else go with us. I don't ever recall my wife asking me to do something like this and could tell that God was using her to speak into a "blind spot" in my life. I assured her that I would either go and take a third party along or not go at all.

Later I explained the situation to my host, telling them how foolish I had been about the whole situation. Thankfully I was able to resolve the matter by having one of them join us. This put to rest any possibility of the enemy exploiting the situation in any way.

In his wonderful book, *The Integrity Crisis*, Warren W. Wiersbe says:

> *What is integrity? The Oxford English Dictionary says that the word comes from the Latin **integritas**, which means "wholeness," "entireness," "completeness." The root word is **integer**, which means "untouched," "intact," "entire." Integrity is to the personal or corporate character what health is to the body or 20/20 vision is to the eyes. A person with integrity is not divided (that's duplicity) or merely pretending (that's hypocrisy). He or she is "whole"; life is "put together," and things are working together harmoniously. People with integrity have nothing to hide and nothing to fear. Their lives are open books. They are integers.*

I had just returned from picking up my mail, in it was the April 2004 issue of *Charisma Magazine*. I began to thumb my way through it while eating my tossed salad and sardine lunch. I quickly glanced at the article under People & Events entitled "Leaders Tackle Tough Integrity Issues." According to the article, some 50 prominent leaders from across the country came together to discuss "issues of moral and financial integrity and the appropriate use of titles especially *apostle* and *prophet*...." Why such a meeting was necessary in the first place is an indictment against the Church.

In his follow-up article, "Challenging Leaders," Stephen Strang writes, "In an age when it seems nearly anything goes—even in the church—and when confrontations about conduct, doctrine, and morality are often greeted with charges of 'judg-mentalism' or 'legalism,' the symposium convened to determine what can be done to set a standard." The article continues, saying, "We saw that too many leaders who are endeavoring to walk in integrity are hurt by extremists—those who by their erroneous teaching or extravagant lifestyles create negative stereotypes for all Charismatics."

"Who shall ascend the hill of the Lord?" David reveals that there are certain requirements necessary if we are to dwell in the presence of God. *"He that walks with integrity and works righteous-ness, he speaks the truth in his heart, he does not slander with his tongue, nor does he do evil to his neighbor, nor take up a reproach against his friend in whose eyes a reprobate is despised, but he honors those who fear the Lord, he swears to his own hurt and he does not change"* (see Ps. 15; Ps. 24).

The one overwhelming requirement for fellowship with God is that of integrity. "He that walks with integrity...works right-eousness...speaks the truth... swears to his own hurt." They keep their word, even though it may cost them everything. They are people you can rely upon—unwavering in their convictions.

Keep Your Promises

Some years ago I was invited to travel down to South America to do some teaching onboard one of the ships belonging to Youth With A Mission (now known as Mercy Ships). The ship was mak-ing its way through the Amazon. Needless to say I was excited to have been asked to go. My mind was already imagining all the amazing sights I'd see as we traveled. I had very few meetings at the time as we had just returned to America from 15 years of min-istry in New Zealand. It wasn't until I checked my calendar that I discovered that I had one meeting that I had committed myself to that fell right in the middle of the time when YWAM needed me on the ship. My first temptation was to try to excuse myself or rearrange the meeting, but I had given my word. I called back to the YWAM office and told them that I was unable to accept the invitation. I've still not seen the Amazon.

Don't Take What Isn't Yours

Paul was a mega-apostle by today's standards, yet instead of constantly appealing for money for "his ministry," he was willing to work. What a novel idea! Writing to the Corinthians he assures them that he has never come by way of deceit, and then elaborates by saying, "I do not seek what is yours." He is referring here to taking their money because he goes on to say, "For children are not responsible to save up for their parents but parents for their children." Paul operated "his ministry" with integrity. He knew how to abound and how to be abased. He wasn't living in a million-dollar mansion then asking the Church to fund "Paul's Apostolic Ministry."

Some years ago when the Lord made it clear that I was to step out in an itinerant ministry, I determined that I would never ask for money either by way of a newsletter or by stating a "fee" for speaking. I also told the Lord that I would never attempt to open doors for meetings. I can testify that for the past six years the Lord has met every need and that I have received ample ministry opportunities both within the United States as well as internationally.

Be an Honest Financial Steward

I have become increasingly shocked, sickened, and saddened by some of the antics used by some in ministry. The "apostles" and "prophets" of today bear little or no resemblance to those of the New Testament. These modern-day wannabes live in the lap of luxury. Many demand to be flown first class and provided with five-star accommodations. They have, for the most part, a single message: Prosperity. Perhaps in some strange way it serves to ease their troubled conscience as they try to bring others into their lavish lifestyle. No, I don't believe that poverty is the answer either, but rather as Paul writes, *"Let your moderation be known unto all men"* (Phil. 4:5).

When the prophet Samuel lay dying, he spoke these words to the nation of Israel: *"...I have walked before you from my youth even to this day. Here I am; bear witness against me before the Lord and His anointed. Whose ox have I taken, or whose donkey have I taken, or whom have I defrauded? Whom have I oppressed, or from whose hand have I taken a bribe to blind my eyes with it? I will restore it to you"* (1 Sam. 12:2-3). The people respond by telling Samuel that he is not guilty of any of these things. What a wonderful man of God who, at the end of his life, can die with a clear conscience. He knows he has not tried to manipulate, defraud, or deceive anyone and that he can die with a clear conscience. What a picture of integrity we see in Samuel!

Desire Integrity in All Areas of Life

There is one verse that still echoes in my ear after hearing it repeatedly over the years from my father: *"A good name is to be more desired than great wealth"* (Prov. 22:1). I cherish hearing that statement from my father. It has kept me focused over the years on what is important: character or cash. I want to have a good name. I want to be a man of integrity. I want it to be known that if I say I'll do something, I'll do it. I want my word to be my bond. I sense that God is looking for those sorts of individuals.

Around a year ago I was asked by my publisher to fly to Canada in order to record several television programs. The other guest who was also being recorded was Gene Edwards. I had read several of his books and was pleased to meet him in person.

I shared with him how for a number of years I had carried in my Bible a page from one of his books. He asked me for it and began to read it. He told me that he had forgotten that he had written it and immediately asked if one of the staff would make him a photocopy.

Allow me to share with you what he had written. He's addressing those who believe that they are being led of the Lord into some type of leadership. He writes:

It would hardly be fair if I did not venture some guess as to what might await you out there on the course, so I will list a few possibilities.

Number 1, a test as to how much you love money.

Number 2, the end of all security.

Number 3, your moral conduct.

Number 4, do you lie? Is the truth important?

Number 5, your willingness to lay down your work and suffer the loss of it all.

Number 6, will you attack another worker or criticize others?

Number 7, will you resort to legalism and fear tactics to hold the work of God together?

Number 8, can you wait until you're 40 or older to begin?

Number 9, can you submit to another worker?

Number 10, can you submit to somebody else's work or one you don't agree with?

Number 11, will you submit to your peers?

Number 12, will you split a work, a church, for any reason? Will you allow others to follow you out of another man's work when you leave it?

Number 13, will you release your own work and leave it forever, giving it into the hands of God?

Number 14, will you serve a lifetime without pay, without money, grow old without a nest egg, do it all with joy and die in poverty without regret?

Number 15, will you work and not be lazy?

Number 16, will you defend yourself when attacked?

Number 17, what will your definition be of a "wolf in our midst," and what will you do with those wolves? [He elaborates on this.]

Number 18, will you keep growing spiritually when you're old?

Number 19, will you have "strong convictions about..." And will you "stand resolutely against..." Because one of the tricks you will learn in the Lord's work is (as I will make note of it later), "that you can hold a work together by teaching your people to hate; a unity based on mutual hate of something or someone."

Number 20, will you give up, will you fall under the withering fire of constant loss, the endless bombardment of discouragement and failure and setbacks?

Number 21, will you get angry at God's people?...for they are slow to learn and quick to forget.

Number 22, will you throw around the teaching of "submission" and "authority"? Men who make issues of these teachings prove that they don't have real authority with God.

Number 23, will you make something other than Christ the centrality of your message, your ministry, and your experience?

Number 24, will all Christians be welcome to share in the fellowship of the Body of Christ regardless of your doctrines?

*Number 25, will you be cowardly or courageous under pressure? Uncompromising? (And you ask, "How can I be meek—give in, submit, walk away from my work—yet be **courageous**?" Ah, dear brother, that is one thing which makes this course so tough!)*

Number 26, can you live with pain, yet never let it break your spirit?

He continues on: "So clean up your life. And crucify the hidden motives of your heart."

I can think of no better list to examine your integrity by than this. Read it over and over again until it takes root in your spirit. You can survive the anointing.

Chapter 13

Unity

Unity without verity [truth] is no better than conspiracy.

—John Trapp

Ah, were their souls fully assured that God had loved them freely, and received them graciously, and justified them perfect-ly, and pardoned them absolutely, and would glorify them ever-lastingly, they could not but love where God loves, and own where God owns, and embrace where God embraces, and be one with every one that is one with Jesus.

—Thomas Brooks

Few things make a mockery of Christianity more than disunity among believers.

—Frederick Coutts,
The Armoury Commentary

U NITY would appear to be one of the most illusive qualities in the Church. The most powerful, passionate, purposeful prayer that Jesus ever prayed was that His people would *"...all be one; even as You, Father, are in Me and I in You, that they also may be in Us, **so that the world may believe** that You sent Me"* (John 17:21).

Little wonder then that the enemy will do everything within his power to keep the Church divided. What staggers me even more is that the Church seems so unaware that disunity is such a major obstacle to reaching the world for Christ. We would far rather "go it alone" than invite others to join us or have us join them. It is this fierce independence that is robbing the Church of blessing. How often we are guilty of quoting Psalm 133:1,3: *"Behold, how good and how pleasant it is for brothers to dwell together in unity!...For there the Lord commanded the blessing—life forever"*; and yet in practice we do everything to avoid one another. I remain convinced that before the Lord returns, these middle walls of partition have to be broken down. God's anointing and blessings will increase upon those who are desirous of fulfilling the "Lord's prayer."

Joseph Brings His Family Together

One of the most beautiful pictures of unity I see in the Bible is in the Book of Genesis. Joseph had been separated from his brethren for some 13 years, during which time the Lord had tested him and promoted him to a position of major influence and authority over the people of Egypt. Eventually the day comes when he is to meet his brothers for the first time in over a decade. Although they don't recognize him, he immediately recognizes them and accuses them of being "spies." They respond by telling Joseph that they are all sons of one man, 12 in all, but that one is no longer and the other is at home with their father. Joseph then informs them that he is going to test them by their own words:

"You shall not go from this place unless your youngest brother comes here" (Gen. 42:15). Simeon is retained by Joseph while the others return to their father.

Once they arrive back at home, Joseph's brothers explain to their father Jacob that there will be no more grain unless Benjamin is allowed to accompany them back to Egypt. Jacob is convinced that he will never see Simeon again and therefore refuses to allow Benjamin to go, fearing this may be the third son to be lost. However, the famine worsens and Jacob is forced to urge his sons to go to Egypt again to buy grain. Judah reminds him, *"The man solemnly warned us, 'You shall **not see my face** unless your brother is with you'"* (Gen. 43:3).

God Wants to Bring His Family Together

There is a greater "Joseph," who possesses greater power and authority, and who is even more desirous of seeing His family brought together and would echo the words of Joseph, "You shall not see *My face* **until** your brothers are with you." That's how much God longs to bring His family together. I believe that when the family of God comes together, when we dwell together in unity, we are going to see the face of God in a way that we've never seen the face of God before.

Whenever we partake of the Lord's Supper, we celebrate the fulfillment of the Old Testament Passover. The Body of Jesus Christ was never to be divided. One of the requirements of the Passover was that when you killed the lamb, you could not break any of its bones.

Jesus' death on the Cross was the fulfillment of the Passover. The soldiers who were responsible for making certain that a crucified man was dead would usually break his leg bones in order to hasten the dying process. The Scriptures tell us that they broke the legs of both men on either side of Jesus but, *"Coming to Jesus, when they saw that He was already dead, they did not break His legs...to fulfill the Scripture, 'Not a Bone of Him Shall Be Broken'"* (John 19:33,36). Surely this was a type of the greater "Body of Christ" that was never to be divided—and yet today the Church remains more fragmented than at any time in history.

We need to earnestly pray for unity. *Lord, bring restoration; bring healing; bring Your Body together. Two are better than one; one will chase a thousand, two 10,000.* The enemy knows that a *"house divided against itself will not stand"* (Matt. 12:25). Therefore the devil will do all within his power to keep us divided.

In closing this chapter, let me say clearly that there is a false unity that is all-embracing—having no standards of morality or integrity, held together by a pseudo love with no foundation of truth or revelation of God. It is solely the work of man and not God.

Chapter 14

Eternity

"A HUNDRED YEARS FROM NOW"

It will not make much difference, friend,
A hundred years from now,
If you lived in a stately mansion
Or a floating river scow.

If the clothes you wear are tailor-made,
Or just pieced together somehow,
If you eat big steaks, or beans, and cake,
A hundred years from now.

Won't matter what your bank account,
What make of car you drive;
For the grave will claim all your riches and fame,
And the things for which you strive.

There's a deadline that we all must meet,
No one will show up late;
It won't matter then, all the places you've been;
Each one will keep that date.

We will only have in eternity,
What we give away on earth.
When we go to the grave, we can only save
The things of eternal worth.

What matter, friend, the earthly gain
For which some men will bow;
For your destiny will be sealed, you see,
A hundred years from now.

—Warren L. Parker

We who live in this nervous age would be wise to meditate on our lives and our days long and often before the face of God and on the edge of eternity. For we are made for eternity as certain as we are made for time, and as responsible moral beings we must deal with both.

—A.W. Tozer

A man's greatest care should be for that place where he lives longest; therefore eternity should be his scope.

—Thomas Manton

ONE of my father's favorite words was the word *"eternity."* Six years ago my wife and I purchased my parents' home here in East Texas. I now have my father's study, which contains 2,000-3,000 books. On the study walls I have several pictures, as well as three plaques with the word "eternity" on them. Not long ago I was speaking to Evangelist Steve Hill and he told me that when he was living in this area my father had called and asked him to make a sign with the word "eternity" on it.

When my wife and I were attending Bible college, we were required to attend the morning chapel times that were held several times a week. Over the platform area there was a large beam, approximately 18 to 20 inches deep. For years the beam had been covered by a banner that read, "Live With Eternity's Values in View." I can still picture that banner now, after more than 40 years.

Paul reveals one of the "keys" to his amazing life and ministry when he writes: *"The things which are seen are temporal, but the things which are not seen are eternal"* (2 Cor. 4:18). That revelation can change your whole course of life. "The things which are seen are *temporal.*" You and I, at best, are going to live for 100 years; but we will spend eternity in the presence of God. Eternity is a long time.

When I was growing up in England, around the age of six or seven, my father was also my pastor. Every Sunday morning he would have the children come forward and sit around the front of the church in order to tell them a story. One of those stories left an indelible impression on my life. My father was attempting to explain to this large group of children the concept of eternity. He began by saying, "Suppose you could find a block of granite one mile square—a mile high, a mile wide, and a mile deep. Now imagine that once every year a little bird comes to that block of granite to sharpen its beak. After sharpening its beak it flies away until the following year when it does the same thing again. This goes on year after year. By the time the block of granite has been worn away, eternity will have just begun." I can still recall thinking, even as a child, that eternity never, ever, ever ends. Hopefully, this simple illustration will serve to challenge you to live your life in the light of eternity.

There is a wonderful song we used to sing as children. The words still convict me even now:

> *Only one life will soon be passed.*
> *Only what's done for Christ will last.*
> *And when I am dying, how glad I shall be*
> *That the lamp of my life*
> *Was burned out for Thee.*

As I have already stated, I believe this was one of the vital "keys" to Paul's life and ministry. He wasn't concerned whether he was in prison, or living like a prince. He testifies, *"I know how to be abased, and I know how to abound, because I've learned in whatever state I'm in to be content"* (see Phil. 4:11-12 NKJV). Paul realized that whether he lived 40 years, 80 years, or 100 years it was nothing in the light of eternity.

This view of eternity seemed to be utmost on his mind when he wrote to the church in Corinth admonishing them to be careful how they lived their lives. He told them that as a wise master builder he had laid a foundation in their lives. He explained that the foundation was Jesus Christ Himself. With the foundation laid, he warned them, they must be careful how they built upon it. This is a very serious portion or passage of Scripture because Paul went on to say that there is coming a day when God Himself would examine every man's work as to what type of life he had lived. Paul says that every man's work will be tested by fire. *"The fire itself will test the quality of each man's work"* (1 Cor. 3:13). Some will suffer a total loss while others will receive a reward.

"Be careful how you build" (see 1 Cor. 3:10) is one of the most severe warnings in the Word of God, because it has eternal consequences to it. Every single one of us will stand one day before the Lord Jesus Christ to give an account of how and for what purpose we have lived our lives. We will stand alone—without the support of a spouse, pastor, friend, or mediator—as our lives subsequent to our salvation is examined by Christ Himself. Our salvation is not on the line here—for salvation is God's gift to each one upon confession of sin and acceptance by faith in Jesus Christ as our Lord and Savior. What *is* at stake is our eternal reward(s).

The Scriptures make it crystal clear that not everyone will be "equal" in Heaven—relationally equal, yes, but not as to our position or rank. That is determined largely by ourselves. Hence Paul's warning, *"Take heed how you build"* (see 1 Cor. 3:10). It was J. Sidlow Baxter who said, "You can have a saved soul but a lost life." In other words we can spend our lives as Christians living simply to please ourselves. Paul, in contrast, states, *"I have as my ambition whether at home or abroad to be pleasing to the Lord"* (see 2 Cor. 5:9). Living in the light of eternity is our safeguard against "a lost life."

Build on Things That Last

Paul exhorts the Corinthians by telling them that they can build in two ways. They can build with gold, silver, and precious stones, or they can use wood, hay, or straw. The latter materials are cheap, common, and plentiful; the former are expensive, small, and rare. Historians tell us that just prior to Paul's writing to the Corinthians, there was a fire (like the great fire of London) that swept through the city of Corinth, resulting in the total destruction of the "shanty town" area of Corinth. Most if not all of this area was filled with houses constructed of wood and other flammable material. The great houses and other stately buildings that survived the fire were constructed of marble or granite, some being decorated with gold and silver. Many believe that these were the precious stones Paul was referring to. To the Corinthians this was "headline news" now being applied by Paul to their Christian walk.

Likewise if we build according to God's plan and purpose for our life, we too can be assured of a reward. Paul himself was convinced of this in respect to his own life. Writing to Timothy, he says: *"I have fought the good fight, I have finished the course, I have kept the faith; in the future there is laid up for me the crown of righteousness, which the Lord, the righteous Judge, will award to me on that day..."* (2 Tim. 4:7-8).

Don't Be Blinded by Worldliness

James Alexander Stewart, the great revivalist evangelist, writes that it is *worldliness* that robs the Christian of their "spiritual eyesight." He says:

> *Worldliness robs the Christian life of its vital radiant dynamic character. Worldliness is anything that takes the keen edge off my spiritual life and dims my vision of the Lord. Worldliness is anything that robs me of my deep inner love-life with my glorious Redeemer. Worldliness is anything that takes away my burden for souls. Worldliness is anything that hinders my spending time in the closet in earnest intercession, by the power of the Spirit, for the church and the world.*
>
> *Whatever passes as a cloud between*
> *The mental eye of faith and things unseen,*
> *Causing that brighter world to disappear,*

Or seem less lovely, or its hope less dear;
***THAT** is our world—our idol, though it bear*
Affection's impress or devotion's air.[1]

He continues, saying, "This worldliness dims the vision of the saints and causes them to lose the sense of eternal value."

As we mature in our calling and ministry we must also increasingly desire the spiritual (unseen) realm, as opposed to the natural (seen) realm. Paul writes, *"For the mind set on the flesh is death, but the mind set on the Spirit is life and peace"* (Rom. 8:6). Notice that it's a mind-set.

This was the key to Jesus' ministry: *"You have loved righteousness and hated lawlessness; **therefore** God, Your God, has **anointed** You"* (Heb. 1:9).

The Japanese now have produced square watermelons—it's true. They have not done it by genetic engineering; they simply place each watermelon in a square plastic mold, and as the watermelon grows, it becomes conformed to the shape of the mold. Paul understood the spiritual significance of this principle when he warned the believers in Rome not to be *"conformed to this world"* but rather *"transformed by the renewing of their minds"* (see Rom. 12:2). Notice again that it has to do with a "mind-set."

Part of that transformation is that we see things from a totally different perspective than the world does. We see things from an eternal vantage point, which in turn should cause us to live our lives from a totally different perspective than that of the world. In the Old Testament we have the tragic story of Esau who traded his (spiritual) birthright for a bowl of chili, so to speak. He was consumed with what he could see and never considered the *unseen,* and thereby he forfeited his future *blessing.* How many believers today follow in the footsteps of Esau, eagerly swallowing every morsel the world offers us without ever considering the tragic eternal consequences?

What am I doing today that counts for eternity? That's what we need to ask ourselves. It changes everything, doesn't it? I want to stand before the Lord one day and hear Him say, *"Well done, thou good and faithful servant"* (Matt. 25:21 NKJV). What is important is not just the fact that you're saved, but that you've served. Not every believer will hear that, only those who have served, only those who have understood the will and the purpose of their Master and have given their lives to accomplish His purpose—to them only will He say, "Well done, good and faithful servant."

Surviving the anointing requires you to live your life in the light of eternity.

Endnote

1. James Alexander Stewart, *Opened Windows: The Church and Revival* (Alexandria, LA: Lamplighter Publications, 1958), 149.

Author Contact Information

For those interested in contacting the author for
speaking engagements, write to:

David Ravenhill
18129 CR 442
Garden Valley, TX 75771

Telephone:
903-882-3942

Website:
www.davidravenhill.net

FAX:
903-882-3740

Personal Notes

Additional copies of this book and other
book titles from DESTINY IMAGE are
available at your local bookstore.

Call toll free: 1-800-722-6774.

Send a request for a catalog to:

Destiny Image₍®₎ Publishers, Inc.

P.O. Box 310
Shippensburg, PA 17257-0310

*"Speaking to the Purposes of God for this
Generation and for the Generations to Come."*

For a complete list of our titles,
visit us at www.destinyimage.com